BREAKTHROUGH

THE RETURN OF HOPE TO THE MIDDLE EAST

TOM DOYLE

Authentic

COLORADO SPRINGS • MILTON KEYNES • HYDERABAD

Authentic Publishing
We welcome your questions and comments.

USA   1820 Jet Stream Drive, Colorado Springs, CO 80921
       www.authenticbooks.com
UK   9 Holdom Avenue, Bletchley, Milton Keynes, Bucks, MK1 1QR
       www.authenticmedia.co.uk
India Logos Bhavan, Medchal Road, Jeedimetla Village, Secunderabad
       500 055, A.P.

Breakthrough: The Return of Hope to the Middle East
ISBN-13: 978-1-934068-63-2

10 09 08 / 6 5 4 3 2 1

A catalog record for this book is available through the Library of Congress.

Cover design: Dan Jamison
Interior design: projectluz.com
Editorial team: Andy Sloan, Dan Johnson, Karen James

Printed in the United States of America

BREAKTHROUGH

Contents

Dedication

This book is dedicated to the saints of God on the spiritual frontlines in the Middle East. God is using them, as their efforts are bringing change to this volatile region. These followers of Christ are in a spiritual war that is raging all around them, yet they will not give up. In fact, they are gaining ground.

This new generation of believers in the Middle East is passionate for God and fearless. Many of them live in poverty, obscurity, and persecution—under the threat of prison or death. Yet because God loves the people of the Middle East and because his saints are faithful, there is a major breakthrough. That is why there is good news coming from the Middle East today.

Breakthrough is an effort to tell that story. It is our privilege to introduce you to these heroes of the faith. Our hope is that you will walk side by side with them, pray for them, and cheer them on.

—Tom Doyle

Acknowledgments

Special thanks to team of researchers for *Breakthrough:*

Dr. Phil Walker
Mom Renda
Tami Thurston
Julia Schatz
Linda Sims
Abraham Sarker
Terry Beh
Lisa Lalani
JoAnn Doyle

1

Can Anything Good Come Out of the Middle East?

The Middle East is the place where history, religion, and politics collide head-on. The lead news story of the day often emanates from this volatile region—and rightfully so, because of its instability. By watching the news on television, it would be easy to form an opinion about the people who live there. It would also be easy to form an opinion about the future of the region, and my guess is that your opinion would not be optimistic. How could it be? Is there ever any good news from the Middle East?

Yes, there *is* good news from the Middle East! In fact, there is *great* news from the Middle East! That is why this book was written. It is time for Christians to find out what is really going on in the Middle East. God is moving in this region in which Jesus was born, ministered, died, and rose again. This book will give you the news that the mainstream media won't give you. Rather than viewing this part of the world with a sense of hopelessness, as we're prone to do, we can celebrate the return of hope.

I'm involved in ministry throughout the Middle East. For the last ten years now I've heard people say, "Tom, you should write a book about all that God is doing in the Middle East."

It's rather ironic that I ended up ministering in this region. The story started with a trip to Israel. In 1995, professors Charlie Dyer and Doug Cecil invited me to join them on a biblical tour of the Holy Land. My initial reaction was that I was too busy, considering that our church was young and growing and I was the senior pastor. But my wife, JoAnn, convinced me that the church could survive without me for ten days. So off I went.

My life was changed. The Bible came alive, and my understanding of Scripture was transformed. Some people in our church even said that my preaching got better when I returned. (I think that's why they were so happy for me to go back each year!)

I not only fell in love with Jesus again while in Israel, but I fell in love with the people there. Both Jews and Arabs found a place in my heart. And I was thrilled to discover that there was a vibrant, growing church in the Middle East. It was also refreshing to see Jews and Arabs who loved each other and had come together in the body of Christ. After four thousand years of strife between Isaac and Ishmael, peace between their descendants seemed too good to be true.

Of course there could be peace between them! I just had never been exposed to the Prince of Peace in action with Jews and Arabs. I didn't even know one Jew or Arab where I lived.

But isn't that what the gospel is all about? Christ came to tear down the wall between Jew and Gentile and to bring peace to both. And I was seeing it. While leading a trip to Israel each year, my love for my Savior and the people of the Middle East grew. I didn't realize it; but after leading a trip to Israel in 2001, my life was about to change dramatically.

Let me back up about a quarter of a century. In 1974, God called me to attend Bible college and then seminary to prepare to be a pastor. It was a dramatic experience as God clearly began to speak to me through important spiritual leaders in my life about going into ministry. Even though I resisted this for a while, God gave me great peace about serving him this way.

I loved being a pastor! How privileged I am to have served Christ in that capacity for over twenty years. I believe there are two things that pastors, as shepherds of God's flock, are responsible to do: feed the flock and lead the flock. I was passionate about fulfilling, through the power of the Spirit of God, both of these responsibilities. For two decades I enjoyed giving maximum effort to these two assignments.

A sense of joy and excitement arrives on Sunday morning when a pastor is ready to teach the Word of God and feed the flock. But there is pressure too. *Do I understand the true meaning of this passage of Scripture? Will I be able to convey God's heart to his followers? Will my application of the biblical text bring hope to those who are hurting today?*

Feeding the flock consistently is not an easy job, to say the least. I can liken preaching a sermon to having a baby. You're excited about the birth, but you don't know what the baby is going to look like. That's how it is with every sermon! Preaching the Bible week in and week out is tough. Each week the pastor's sermon is analyzed and critiqued. But more important for the preacher is answering the question, *Did I faithfully bring God's Word to his people today?* Being called to teach the Bible and make it relevant to God's people is a high honor and privilege.

Leading the flock is also an honor, though it will drain a pastor of every ounce of energy. There are highs and lows. One week you may experience the joy of performing a wedding; the next week you may be called upon to perform a funeral. Like feeding the flock, leading the flock is not an easy job. People have problems. They die. Their marriages fail. Their children walk away from God. Then the pastor is called in to help God's followers get through the crisis. How awesome to bring God's love and compassion to his people in time of need. Only God can heal the hurts and give his people the strength to make it through the difficult trials of life. The pastor gets to see this up close and often. This too is a privilege.

Go East, Young Man!

This was the world in which I lived. This was my calling, and I thought that I would be feeding and leading the flock for the rest of my life. But on the first Sunday in June 2001, God called again. I had just preached a sermon at my church, Tri-Lakes Chapel in Monument, Colorado; and while we were worshiping near the end of the service, God began to speak to my heart. The message was clear: *This is the last sermon you will preach at Tri-Lakes Chapel.*

This impression came across so clearly that I responded, *Lord, is that you? Or am I imagining this?* I was in a state of shock. The people sitting nearby must have thought, *Is the pastor having some kind of meltdown? He's just staring straight ahead!*

I left the service shaken and immediately headed for my wife, JoAnn. JoAnn and I have been married for twenty-eight years. She is an amazing wife, mother of our six children, and now grandmother. She also has an insight into people and situations of which I am often clueless. I said, "JoAnn, the strangest thing just happened. I think God told me that we are going to leave the church. I don't understand this, do you?"

"Yes, I do!" she replied immediately. "Over the last few months I have felt that God was beginning to release us from Tri-Lakes into another ministry field altogether. Let me ask you a question. If you weren't a pastor, how would you want to serve God?"

I thought for a moment and then said, "I think it would be in missions."

JoAnn then asked, "And where do you think that would be?"

That was an easy one. "In Israel and the Middle East."

"So do I!" JoAnn replied. "Tom, I believe that God is calling us to leave local church ministry and to serve him on the frontlines in missions."

We didn't waste any time. The next day I went to the elders and told them what was on our hearts. Wanting to make sure this wasn't just a whim, they graciously counseled me to take three weeks off and seek the Lord. That was great advice, and I will always thank the Lord for their godly direction. Those three weeks were pivotal in our spiritual journey. Both JoAnn and I began to sense God's calling so strongly that it erased any doubts that we might have had previously.

Making the jump from pastor to missionary sounded like some sort of midlife crisis to some of our friends, and not all of them were as enthusiastic as we were. But God was burning into our hearts a call to go to the mission field. We lived in the Colorado Springs area, where well over a hundred ministry organizations are located. Many staff members of those organizations went to our church. With so many great ministries in existence, how were we to know which one to join? We needed direction from God—and that direction would come quickly.

A longtime friend, Curtis Hail, called and said that he was going to be in our area and wanted to drop by for a visit. Curtis had served in missions for about fifteen years, and I had been on mission trips with him to the Soviet Union and Argentina. Curtis and Nathan Sheets had just formed a new ministry called EvangeCube. Curtis stunned us when he said, "We're looking for a Middle East director—someone who will work with pastors."

JoAnn and I broke into laughter. "Are you serious? That is exactly what we believe God is calling us to do!"

When God is in something, he sure knocks down the barriers. We have found that those barriers often are not real but only in our minds. After some concentrated prayer, we knew that God had opened the door for us at EvangeCube, which later changed its name to e3 Partners.

At the end of June, we said goodbye to our church, after nine wonderful years of ministry. I was supposed to preach a farewell sermon, but in both services I broke down and began crying. I couldn't get any words out. I felt so badly that I wasn't able to preach one last message to these people I dearly loved. But JoAnn reminded me that God had clearly impressed on my heart on that first Sunday in June: *This is the last sermon you will preach at Tri-Lakes Chapel.*

My days as a pastor were now over. It was on to the mission field!

The next few months were dedicated to raising support for our new ministry. The thought of raising support was intimidating and funny at the same time. As a senior pastor, I loved missions; and missions became a major part of our church life. But I had often said, "I don't know how our missionaries do it. I could never raise support. With six kids, that would be insane!" Ironically, that is exactly what God called us to do. And we soon found out that his ability to provide is more than we can imagine. He has been so faithful.

Middle Eastern Terrorism Goes Global

Within a couple of months, something happened that changed everything in our new ministry.

As I was driving home after dropping off our daughter at school, ABC News interrupted the radio station I was listening to with this: "An airplane has gotten off course and has just slammed into the World Trade Center." Since I had led tours to Israel and Jordan, I was tuned into the terrorism threats that emanated continually from the region. My first thought was *There are no flight patterns through Manhattan—this is a terrorist attack!*

When I got home and turned on the TV, JoAnn and I saw the second plane hit the World Trade Center. America was under attack.

After the four coordinated strikes, the country was in shock. The stories of those who had lost their lives were devastating. This tragedy woke us up to the fact that we had enemies who were calling for our nation's destruction. I remember being glued to the television and watching Fox News go live to the Gaza Strip where crowds cheered in the streets over al-Qaeda's attack on us. As the drama unfolded over the next several days, I wondered more than a few times how we could ever go to the very places that were the hotbed of Islamic fundamentalism.

I wasn't the only one who had questions. Here are a few of the questions we were asked after 9/11: "Won't you be killed if you go to the Middle East?" "They hate Americans in all the Muslim countries. Can't you go somewhere else?" "Are you sure that God didn't say the *Far* East instead of the *Middle* East?!" "How can you even think of going there with your wife and six children?" (That last one really hurt.)

And these were the comments just from our relatives!

As the days went by, however, JoAnn and I came to the realization that this was indeed the time to be involved in missions in the Middle East. We realized that it is normal for us Americans to typecast people. "We're the good guys and they're the bad guys. We wear the white hats and they wear the black hats." It would be easy to conclude from the news that all Muslims are terrorists (and watch out if you ever see them—because they probably have bombs strapped to their bodies). But the Muslims we met in Israel and in Jordan were far from that. They were just normal people. We had friends who practiced Islam, and they didn't hate us or the West.

More important than that is the fact that people in the Middle East are created in the image of God, just like everyone else in the world. They need and deserve to be reached with the good news of Jesus Christ, who died for their sins as well as for ours. JoAnn and I weren't naive. There was no question in our minds that Islamic fundamentalism is a threat to global security. And if we wanted to share Christ in the Middle East, of course there would be dangers. But that didn't erase the Great Commission of Matthew 28, in which Jesus commanded us as his followers to "go and make disciples of all nations." Notice that Jesus didn't say to "go and make disciples of the nations that like you and are relatively friendly."

The Door Is Open

A good friend of mine in Jerusalem recently said, "As believers, we often hear people say, 'These people are open to the claims of Christ,' or 'The door is wide open in this country for the gospel.' But I don't see that as a biblical concept. The question is: Are *we* open to sharing the gospel?"

I agree. After all, Jesus promised, "On this rock I will build my church, and the gates of Hades will not overcome it" (Matthew 16:18). In other words, with Jesus all doors are open.

He has sent the church to all nations, no matter what the current trends appear to be. I believe we can get into any nation with the good news of Jesus Christ. And there is a new generation of Christians in the Middle East today who believe, deep in their hearts, that with Jesus all doors are open. In reality, if you don't have that attitude, it would be easy to give up and quit.

So, in 2001 we joined a group of believers in various ministries who were passionate about sharing the life-changing message of Jesus Christ in the Middle East. I have personally seen that Muslims in the Middle East, and throughout the rest of the Muslim world, are eager to hear about Jesus.

Since I began traveling extensively in the Middle East, I have also learned that the vast majority of Muslims are peaceful and not into jihad. They just want to feed their children, send them to good schools, see them get married, and enjoy a houseful of grandchildren running around their home when they break the fast each evening during Ramadan. From Egypt to Iran, the Muslims we talk to are sick of the Islamic fundamentalism that isolates them from the world and makes them all out to be bloodthirsty killers. We must reach out and love these people with the love of Jesus.

Arthur Blessitt has carried a large wooden cross in every country of the world. That amazes me, and it also makes me proud that someone would have the nerve to do such a thing. Showing up with a cross in some places on the globe could get you killed. Arthur has been in such danger many times. I am honored to call Arthur a friend. When I am with him, he always reminds me: "Tom, just keep it about Jesus! That is our message, and it's a simple one. Once we get off of that, we lose people."

How true that is. As we soon found out in our ministry in the Middle East, Muslims were ready to talk about Jesus. We also found out that they weren't all calling for the destruction of America.

I remember walking through the streets of the Gaza Strip a few months after 9/11 when a woman in an *abaya* approached me.

"You're from America, aren't you?" she asked. "I can tell by your blue eyes."

"Yes, I am."

She continued: "Did you see on the news the people in Gaza celebrating in the streets when the buildings collapsed in New York City?"

"I am afraid I did," I replied sadly.

"Well, I wasn't cheering. I was crying for all of those families who lost their loved ones. That was a tragedy, and many of the Muslim people were grieving with you."

With that, the woman walked away. She obviously needed to get this off her mind, and I was glad to be the one to hear it. I believe God prearranged this conversation for my sake and for the sake of the small group with me. Here was this woman reaching out to me, which would have been considered out of bounds since she was a practicing Muslim. But she did it anyway.

I thought to myself, *We can work with these people!* This woman's message showed that she cared and that not all Muslims want to wipe out the West. Her heart came through, and I could see her grief as she recounted the tragedy that America had just endured.

Why *Breakthrough*?

I have been privileged, over the years, to minister in Israel—including the Palestinian territories in the West Bank and the Gaza Strip—Iran, Syria, Egypt, Iraq, Lebanon, Jordan, the United Arab Emirates, and Afghanistan. Some of the books I have read recently about the Middle East were written by people who don't spend much time there but were merely reacting to the news they hear on television or on the Internet. But there is so much more—a story that is not being told, in my opinion. Since I work in the Middle East, I am privileged to see this story unfold time after time. The story is this: *Jesus is reaching out to the people of the Middle East in a powerful way, and the people are responding in record numbers. Millions have given their lives to Jesus Christ in the last ten years.*[1] *That's right—millions!*

This story is more important than the latest suicide bombing, the latest threat of war, or the latest prophecy about Jesus' return. Of course I believe all of those things are important; but often lost in all of that is the fact that Jesus is building his church in the Middle East and that it is filled with former Muslims.

Maybe Jesus will return in our lifetime. How humbling it is to ponder that we could be the chosen generation that welcomes his arrival. But if biblical prophecies point to that, then we, as Jesus' church, need to be making the greatest effort

---

1. Joel C. Rosenberg, *Epicenter: Why the Current Rumblings in the Middle East Will Change Your Future* (Carol Stream, IL: Tyndale, 2006), 211.

to reach the world with his message. Once Jesus returns, it will be too late.

One of the most important regions of the world is the Middle East. After all, this is where the church was birthed. For centuries the church has been small and almost unnoticed. We can no longer say that, however. Jesus is not being ignored in the Middle East today. The new generation of believers who serve Christ is willing to give their lives to make sure that everyone has an opportunity to hear of Jesus' offer of grace and forgiveness. They are willing to risk everything to make sure new believers have a Bible and can grow in their new life in Christ. They put themselves in harm's way daily as they start new churches in places that have had no Christian presence for centuries.

In our work in the Middle East we have met some of the most godly, loving, and committed believers we have encountered any place in the world. They are constantly watched and often persecuted. They have a special calling as they live with the understanding that today might be their last day. Yet they often state, "We pray for you believers in the West every day."

Many of the leaders we work with were at one time terrorists. In the following chapters you will be introduced to many of them. God miraculously transformed them, and they will never be the same. Their testimonies remind us of two things:

1. No one is unreachable . . . not even a terrorist.
2. The worst place to be a believer is really the best place to be a believer.

That second statement may be puzzling to you, like it was to me the first time I heard it. It simply means this: *The most dangerous places to serve Christ are usually the places where he is moving the most.* We have found that to be true. The light of God shines brightest in the darkness. When people are living in the midst of war, poverty, terrorism, and desperation, God then becomes their only hope. How miserable is an existence without hope, and Jesus is bringing hope to this troubled region.

So can anything good come out of the Middle East? Yes! And, in a sense, you are about to go there. It's time for you to meet these heroes of our faith and discover the hope that has returned to this part of the world. Even more important than that is to see firsthand God's love and power on display in the place where history, religion, and politics collide. Because of enormous security risks, in most cases the names in these stories will be changed. In some instances, places will be changed also. We want to protect the leaders at all costs and make sure that this book is a blessing to them, too.

Breakthrough will now take a look at how Islam began and where the religion finds itself today. I aim to be both accurate in my presentation of history and respectful of Muslims. I have a deep love for the Muslim people, and I am committed to reaching them with the love of Jesus. I am not interested in slamming either them as a people or the religion of Islam. Again, I believe we are called to keep the message about Jesus. I believe our most powerful weapon is the love that comes from our Savior, who loved us and gave his life for us on the cross. We did nothing to deserve his love for us, but he showered it upon us nonetheless.

As you read this book, I pray that God will open your heart with love for the people of Islam. With that in mind, let's journey together into the Middle East.

2

Out of the Desert— The Birth of Islam

Where It All Started: Mecca, Arabia, AD 570

When he was forty years old, he began to have bizarre, frightening visions and dreams. Muhammad, the son of Abdullah of Mecca, wondered what all this might mean. Was he demonized? Was he crazy? His wife had a different opinion: she believed he was a prophet of God. Muhammad began a new religion. And the rest, as they say, is history. Islam was born.

Muhammad and Khadija were married in AD 595. Her belief that he was a true prophet of God would change the course of countless nations and affect the lives of over one billion people. And that's just how the religion affects the world today. For centuries Islam has made its way around the world. But to fully understand it, we must travel back in time and back to the place where it began.

In the sixth century, Mecca, Arabia, was home to several pagan religions and idols: 360 of them, in fact—one for each day of the lunar year. The people of the desert, it seems, were fervently committed to their gods. The idolatry accompanying this paganism was so well developed that it became the most lucrative business in all of the Arabian Desert.[1]

In AD 570, Muhammad was born into this center of pagan worship. His father, Abdullah, died while his mother, Amina, was pregnant with Muhammad. Amina then died when he was only six years old. Muhammad was taken in by an uncle. He would never be accused of being lazy, as he entered the merchant world at a young age. At the age of twelve he traveled with his uncle to Damascus, Syria.

When Muhammad was twenty-five, he married Khadija, a forty-year-old widow. Fifteen years later, in 610, Muhammad experienced what Khadija called his first "revelation," marking the beginning of his life as "the prophet of God."[2]

The spiritual landscape of the area during those days was quite different from today's Middle East. By the time Muhammad was born, Jews had been worshiping Yahweh for nearly 2,700 years. The glorious history of the chosen people began when Abraham entered the land of Canaan around 2100 BC. The

---

1. Abraham Sarker, *Understand My Muslim People* (Newberg, OR: Barclay Press, 2004), 37.
2. Don Richardson, *Secrets of the Koran: Revealing Insights into Islam's Holy Book* (Ventura, CA: Regal Books, 2003), 31.

not-so-glorious history of the chosen people ended when the descendants of Abraham were kicked out of the land in AD 70. I believe Scripture clearly indicates that God was not finished with the Jews and that one day they would return to their precious land of Canaan (Isaiah 66:8; Ezekiel 37; Zechariah 8:1–8).

But when Muhammad was born, the Jews had been dismissed from Israel and dispersed to a multitude of nations for five hundred years. Jesus himself prophesied this exodus from Israel during his triumphal entry into Jerusalem at the beginning of the last week of his earthly life.

> As he approached Jerusalem and saw the city, he wept over it and said, "If you, even you, had only known on this day what would bring you peace—but now it is hidden from your eyes. The days will come upon you when your enemies will build an embankment against you and encircle you and hem you in on every side. They will dash you to the ground, you and the children within your walls. They will not leave one stone on another, because you did not recognize the time of God's coming to you." (Luke 19:41–44)

Because of the Jews' rejection of "God's coming to [them]" through Jesus Christ, the Messiah, the horrific Roman invasion would occur within forty years. Jerusalem would be destroyed, and the Jews who survived would be scattered from the land for centuries. By the time Muhammad was born, Jews were living in many parts of the world—including Mecca in present-day Saudi Arabia.

Another important spiritual dynamic at the time of Muhammad's birth was the condition of Christianity. With five centuries of phenomenal growth behind it, the church had moved into a different phase. The evangelistic fire was now cooling, and doctrinal debates were in full swing. The church had dealt with controversies concerning the deity of Christ and the nature of the Trinity, important issues to say the least. Yet these matters, along with the church's emerging hierarchy, had a paralyzing effect on evangelism. In short, the church turned inward instead of outward.

So both Jews and Christians were living in Mecca when Muhammad was born, though neither of them were at the zenith of their influence.

Pagans were also spread throughout the Middle East, and Arab pagan religions flourished in the desert during this time. Pre-Islamic history is a subject that Muslim scholars avoid as much as possible, since so much of their religion clearly has been borrowed from Arabian paganism during the formation of the Koran and Islam itself.[3]

The holiest site of Islam is the Black Stone of Kaaba, located in Mecca. This stone is to the Muslim what the temple mount in Jerusalem is to the Jew. As Christians, biblical sites naturally are special to us. The Sea of Galilee, where Jesus lived and performed the majority of his miracles during his earthly ministry, is one of them. The Mount of Olives, where Jesus prayed and from where he ascended to heaven, is another. But for believers, prayer is not

---

3. Robert Morey, "Christianity's Response to Islam," lecture presented at New Life Orthodox Presbyterian Church, La Mesa, CA, October 2001.

location driven. Prayers in the name of Jesus have equal value whether they are prayed in New York City or Jerusalem. Not so for Muslims. So important are the prayers in Mecca that a Muslim's eternal destiny depends on it.

The same was true before Islam began. The only difference at that time was that the Kaaba Stone was shared by 360 religions instead of just one. Once every year, the followers of each of these pagan religions assembled and circled around the big black meteorite in prayer. This festival was the desert event of the year.[4]

A Reluctant Leader Emerges: Muhammad and the Cave

Mecca was a small western Arabian town; but since it had an oasis, it became a popular stop for desert caravans. The town was often filled with a strange combination of raiding tribes, nomads, and pagan worshipers. Many of the people in the area made a living raising camels, sheep, and goats. Others worked the soil in the few places in the harsh desert where crops could grow. Still others worked in the trading business. Mecca began to experience rapid growth, and the town began to change.

In the fortieth year of his life, Muhammad was worried. He believed that Mecca was turning into nothing more than a wealthy trading post. Though small, Mecca was the most important place for Arab pagan worship. After all, Arab legend taught that civilization began here. The cube-shaped Kaaba shrine

---

4. Sarker, *Understand My Muslim People*, 37.

claimed a very ancient history. The local people believed that the Kaaba was built by Adam, the first created human being, and rebuilt by Ibrahim (Abraham) the prophet and his son Ishmael. But now it was quickly becoming a center for commerce and corruption.[5]

As was his habit every year during the month of Ramadan, Muhammad entered a cave just outside Mecca to pray and fast. He also would give alms to the poor while in Mecca. This strange, dark night in that cave on Mount Hira on the seventeenth night of the month began a period of Muhammad's life that would last for twenty-one years.

In her best-selling book *Islam*, Karen Armstrong, a specialist in world religions, writes, "The revelations were painful to Muhammad, who used to say: 'Never once did I receive a revelation without thinking that my soul had been torn away from me.' In the early days, the impact was so frightening that his whole body was convulsed; he would often sweat profusely, even on a cool day, experience a great heaviness, or hear strange sounds and voices."[6]

An entity arrived, identifying himself as Jibril—or Gabriel, as we say in English. He claimed to be an angel and instructed Muhammad to read his words and recite them back. There was only one problem: like the majority of people in the desert, Muhammad was illiterate. According to Islamic folklore it didn't matter, however, because a miracle supposedly happened at that

---

5. Karen Armstrong, *Islam: A Short History* (New York: Modern Library, 2000), 3.
6. Ibid., 3.

point. Muhammad was instantly given the ability to read and write. The man who couldn't read or write moments before was now being entrusted with a new revelation for the world to hear and read.

So frightening were the visions that Muhammad shared them with only two people for the first couple of years. He confided in his wife, Khadija, and her cousin Waraqa, who claimed to be a Christian.

So just what were these encounters? Since Muslims believe Muhammad had a direct line to Allah, they overlook the bizarre effect these dreams and visions had on their leader. Today Muslims talk openly about the Prophet foaming at the mouth and being covered with a sheet when the revelations came to him. He would immediately fall to the ground, and his convulsions would continue during the entire time the message was being delivered.[7]

In Afghanistan a few years ago an imam became highly esteemed because his pronouncements came after a Muhammad-like trance, complete with foaming at the mouth and convulsions. According to Muslim scholars, he was following the path of the Prophet himself, whose manifestations became the major evidence of his credibility.

Today doctors would probably conclude that Muhammad had epilepsy. The characteristics are identical to those who suffer with this crippling disease. Many conclude that Muhammad merely needed a good doctor. But what if the situation pointed to something else?

---

7. Sarker, *Understand My Muslim People*, 46.

Muhammad and Moses:
Two Peas in a Pod?

I believe that Muhammad's condition was spiritually related. He was convinced of this himself, at least for a while. It seems the presence of evil was so strong that Muhammad believed he had become demon-possessed. Abraham Sarker, in his helpful book *Understand My Muslim People*, opens this Pandora's box on the origin of Muhammad's inspiration.

> At first he felt very distressed, believing an evil spirit had possessed him. He felt deathly afraid of the source of this new revelation. Respected modern Muslim biographer, M. H. Haykal, describes Muhammad's fear: "Stricken with panic, Muhammad arose and asked himself, 'What did I see? Did possession of the devil which I feared all along come to pass?' Muhammad looked to his right and then his left and saw nothing. For a while he stood there trembling with fear and stricken with awe. He feared the cave might be haunted and he might run away, still unable to explain what he saw."[8]

So we see that Muhammad's initial reaction was one of terror, as he feared that the angelic visitor was from Satan. On the other hand, when the prophets of the Old Testament witnessed the presence of God, their reactions were quite different.

Genesis 12 records that Abraham was called by God to leave his homeland and go to a place God would later reveal to him. He left and followed God with no questions asked.

---

8. Ibid., 44–45.

We see in Exodus 3 that when God spoke to Moses from the burning bush, Moses responded by saying, "Here I am." He then accepted God's call on his life, even if it was reluctantly.

Isaiah 6 tells us of this great prophet's call. Isaiah, well aware that the Lord was revealing himself to him, also felt acutely aware of his own personal sin. "Woe to me! . . . I am ruined!" But then he responded affirmatively to God's call: "Here am I. Send me!"

Jeremiah was also called by God personally. As we see in the first chapter of Jeremiah's book, the Lord informed him that before he was even born he had been called to be a prophet to the nations. Like Moses, Jeremiah claimed he didn't know how to speak—contending that he was too young. God charged Jeremiah not to be afraid, and then he reached out and touched Jeremiah's mouth. From then on the young prophet was a power-house for God.

When Gabriel Visited

So how about Gabriel's visitations recorded in the Bible? Do they resemble the visitation that Muhammad experienced?

Daniel 8 shows us that the angel Gabriel approached the prophet Daniel to explain the puzzling vision he had about a ram and a goat. Like Muhammad, Daniel initially was frightened, falling on his face before the angel. Gabriel went on to tell Daniel what the strange vision meant. Daniel 9 recounts another vision, but this one occurred about a dozen years later. Again Daniel was approached by Gabriel. This time, however, his reaction was quite different. Daniel experienced no fear when Gabriel arrived and explained the vision of seventy "sevens."

In the New Testament, in the first chapter of Luke's Gospel, Gabriel announced the birth of both John the Baptist and Jesus. Gabriel first visited Zechariah, a priest who, along with his wife, Elizabeth, lived in a town in the hill country of Judea. Zechariah had been chosen by lot to go into the temple at Jerusalem and minister to the Lord. While Zechariah was burning incense in the Holy Place, Gabriel suddenly appeared. Zechariah, of course, was gripped with fear.

Luke 1:6 states that both Zechariah and Elizabeth were upright in God's sight, so why was Zechariah surprised that the Lord would send his messenger to the holiest place on the face of the earth? I believe it's because Israel had just endured four hundred years of silence. At the close of the Old Testament, God was so frustrated with the entire nation that he cut off communication with his chosen people. No prophets, no word from heaven. When Gabriel arrived, the priests had been going through the motions for four centuries. Zechariah wasn't exactly expecting a message from God, let alone an angelic visit in the temple. No wonder he was afraid.

Next Gabriel visited Mary, who lived in Nazareth, a town in Galilee. Mary wondered why he would burst in and say, "Greetings, you who are highly favored! The Lord is with you" (Luke 1:28). Gabriel explained to Mary the amazing privilege God was giving her. It involved a miracle that would become known as the virgin birth. Mary was called to serve God in a unique way, a way unlike anyone before or after her. Mary responded to the plan laid out by the angelic visitor: "I am the

Lord's servant. . . . May it be to me as you have said" (Luke 1:38).

In each of Gabriel's three visitations in the Bible, Daniel, Zechariah, and Mary were amazed at the importance of the situation and that God had chosen them to be a part of it. Mary was not fearful, nor was Daniel on Gabriel's second visit. Zechariah was stunned and shocked, but obedient nonetheless.

When God Visited

In Scripture, prophets, priests, and kings were called by God at various times throughout the history of Israel. In almost every case they experienced similar responses.

We see in Exodus 3 and 4 that Moses felt he didn't have the ability to communicate clearly. His fear was people centered; he didn't believe the Israelites—let alone Pharaoh—would listen to him. God demonstrated that the persuasive power Moses needed was with the Lord, not with Moses. Over time, Moses' fear evaporated (see Exodus 14:13–14). God's presence and power were so undeniable that it became clear there really wasn't anything for him to worry about.

Isaiah was willing to serve God; but when he was ushered into the Lord's throne room, he was overwhelmed by his own sinful nature. Isaiah was on his face before God, but all he could see was the evil in his life. The scene was majestic. The angels known as seraphs were hovering over the Lord as he sat on his throne in all of his glory. The train of God's robe filled the whole room. Isaiah was in the presence of "the Holy One of Israel." The sound of the angelic worship shook the room, and Isaiah was "undone," as one translation puts it in Isaiah 6:5.

Jeremiah claimed he was unable to represent God because of his youthfulness. Jeremiah cries out, "Ah, Sovereign LORD, . . . I do not know how to speak; I am only a child" (Jeremiah 1:6). Actually he was probably in his early twenties but nonetheless felt wholly inadequate to represent God before his chosen people.

Moses and Jeremiah were in the top tier of prophets. They learned soon enough that their inadequacy was overcome by the nature of God and his sheer power. Isaiah needed to know that his "unclean lips" would be forgiven by God. He was forgiven, and today he is generally considered the prophet of all prophets in the Bible. Abraham appears at first to have had no such fear but later displayed it when he tried to "help" God bring about an heir. God intended Isaac to be the firstborn all along, but Abraham and Sarah believed they needed to make it happen—so along came Ishmael. Abraham's fear was that God couldn't pull it off.

So Abraham, Moses, Isaiah, and Jeremiah were all fearful when God approached them. Their reluctance was either because of feelings of inadequacy for the task or, in Isaiah's case, because of personal sin that was magnified in the awesome presence of God.

Is Muhammad Just Part of the Gang?

So how does Muhammad's experience compare to those of the prophets of the Bible? Muhammad claimed to be called by

Jibril, which is Arabic for Gabriel. This means that the same angel who spoke directly to Daniel in the Old Testament and to Zechariah and Mary in the New Testament supposedly met Muhammad in the cave outside of Mecca.

Gabriel is one of two angels mentioned by name in the Bible. The other is Michael. They play different but important roles. Michael the archangel is the warrior angel who fights for God and defends God's people, as seen in Daniel 10:13 and 12:1. Gabriel is the angel who represents God to his people and brings them specific messages.

The impact of Muhammad receiving a visitation from Gabriel would have caused people to give this new religion a serious look. If Gabriel did indeed visit Muhammad, the accompanying revelation would link together Judaism, Christianity, and Islam and validate the claim that the new faith was really built on the foundation of the other two. Satan could not have played a more strategic card.

Is there a difference between Muhammad's encounter and those of Abraham, Moses, Isaiah, Jeremiah, Daniel, Zechariah, and Mary? Yes, there is a major difference; and the comparison is startling. Remember, Muhammad himself spoke of his fear of being possessed by the Devil. Living in one of the most paganized areas of the world, the possibility of this happening was all too probable. The apostle Paul said, in 1 Corinthians 10:20, that sacrifices made to idols are in reality offered to demons. Living in Mecca, Muhammad was swimming in demonic activity. With 360 idols worshiped openly and routinely there, the spiritual warfare was intense to say the least.

I believe that Muhammad's initial encounter with "Gabriel" was a classic example of demon possession. He described being physically crushed as he spoke with the angel in the midst of the "revelation." Muhammad said the angel squeezed him so tight in the cave outside of Mecca that he thought he would die.[9] Demon possession involves fear and intimidation, as the evil spirit overwhelms the person into submission. In subsequent visitations, Muhammad experienced several other intimidating physical manifestations, such as headaches, foaming at the mouth, and the hearing of bells to announce another vision.[10]

The most important difference between the visitations recorded in the Bible and Muhammad's visitations is this: *Not once in Scripture did anyone ever confuse the call of God with the call of Satan.* There was fear, but that fear was based on the incredible and awesome presence of God. When God or Gabriel spoke, no one ever said: "I wonder if this is God or Satan." In all cases the call of God was so convincing, so conclusive, and so authoritative that the recipients were immediately convinced, as were those around them. There was no question about who originated the vision.

In Matthew 12:31–32, Jesus said that blasphemy against the Spirit will not be forgiven, either in this age or in the age to come. I believe the unpardonable sin is attributing the works of God to Satan. Confusing God's works with Satan's works is as far out of bounds as anyone can ever go.

Two options are possible:

---

9. Ibid., 46.
10. Ibid.

1. Muhammad was right when he wondered if the angel was from Satan.

2. Muhammad was wrong when he interpreted God's works as Satan's.

If Muhammad was right and the angel was from Satan, then a false religion began in the cave that day—a religion inspired by none other than Satan himself. If Muhammad was wrong when he interpreted God's works as Satan's, then another problem arises. If Islam is truly built on the foundation of Judaism and Christianity, then Muhammad trapped himself by initially attributing the "angelic vision" to the Devil. If this is the case, then I believe that Muhammad, by his own admission, committed blasphemy against the Spirit. This then means there was no way he could ever enter into heaven. Muhammad loses either way.

Muhammad's first response to the troubling vision he received was most definitely the correct one. Paul tells us, in 2 Corinthians 11:14, that Satan "masquerades as an angel of light." Muhammad originally believed that the angel who appeared to him in that cave was evil. The evidence could not have been clearer. Muhammad's vision was nothing like those of the prophets of the Bible. It could not compare to Gabriel's visitation to Zechariah. Nor could it compare to the vision that Mary had when Gabriel announced the coming birth of Jesus. The comparisons that Islamic apologists often give to position Muhammad into the biblical line of the prophets comes up short no matter how you look at them. In short, it appears that Muhammad's wife, Khadija, gave him the worst advice of his life.

BREAKTHROUGH

Her advice was followed, however, and a new religion was established. The revelations continued, and now they would need to be recorded. Muhammad put his book together, and to Muhammad's followers it is the holiest of all books. The very words of this book are considered sacred, having hypnotic effects on Muslims both yesterday and today. This book has 114 Suras, or chapters, and each Sura contains several verses. Together these Suras form the book known as the Koran.

3

From Revelation to Religion

Muhammad and the Jews: Round One in Mecca

Muhammad first took his message to the people of Mecca. A small number of Jews lived in the city; and even though this certainly was not a hotbed of Judaism, they were still practicing their religion. The nation of Israel had dissolved some 540 years before, as the Jews were scattered over the face of the earth. The long history of Judaism included both true prophets and false prophets. Would these Jews listen to Muhammad or reject him?

BREAKTHROUGH

The Jews in Mecca responded to Muhammad in the latter fashion. After all, they were a small minority group in the midst of numerous Arabic tribes that were rooted in idolatry. The odds of being able to stand up and make their objections heard were slim. In addition, these Jews had a relatively good standing in the community, and many of them had become wealthy because of their business skills. So why rock the boat (or tip over the camel)? They chose instead to be passive and have no opinion about the young leader in search of credibility.

A Jewish endorsement right out of the chute would have been huge for Muhammad, but these descendants of Abraham weren't interested. Muhammad's first Jewish evangelistic campaign was a bust that resulted in zero converts. He enlisted a few Arab followers, but the majority of the people of Mecca rejected him—and persecuted him to make sure he got the point. Muhammad wasn't welcome in his hometown anymore.[1]

I'll bet I know what you're thinking. *It's hard to believe that Muhammad would have even cared what the Jews thought about him.* Or *Why would Muhammad be the least bit concerned about whether the Jews believed in his "visions" that made up the Koran? After all, Jews and Arabs were sworn enemies for centuries—millennia. That's how it has always been, right?*

Wrong! Amazingly, the Middle East was vastly different in AD 613. In fact, when Muhammad hit the scene, Jews and Arabs were living together peacefully. Synagogues had been built throughout the Arabian Peninsula. Years before, these cousins

---

1. Bernard Lewis, *The Middle East: A Brief History of the Last 2,000 Years from the Rise of Christianity to the Present Day* (New York: Scribner, 1995), 52.

had given up their long-standing hostility toward each other and were experiencing a calm coexistence in many Arabic cities and villages.[2]

Jewish persecution during this period typically was not at the hands of the Arabs. The majority of hatred leveled at the Jews during this time came from Christians. Some early church fathers spoke openly about their animosity toward Jews, claiming that the Jews killed the Messiah and that it was the duty of the church to make them pay for it. John Chrysostom ministered in the latter part of the fourth century. He was the patriarch of the church in Constantinople. Not only that, but he was born in Antioch, which Acts 11:26 tells us was where followers of Jesus Christ were first called Christians. The most eloquent preacher of his day, he was called "Chrysostom," meaning "golden mouthed," because of his tremendous ability to communicate the truths of Scripture. He was such a powerful preacher that he often had to rebuke people for applauding in church, which was considered inappropriate in those days. Chrysostom had it all. And what did he think of the Jews? His three simple words said it all: "Kill the pigs!" In those days, the main battlefront for Jews was the church.[3]

So in Muhammad's early years the Jews of the Arabian Desert were living in relative peace with the Arabs, with reason to believe this would continue for many years. Once Muhammad moved to Medina, however, the Jews would think that Christian

---

2. Ibid., 47.

3. David Dolan, *Israel at the Crossroads: Fifty Years and Counting* (Grand Rapids: Revell, 1998), 30–41.

persecution was a cakewalk compared to what the new religion was ready to dish out.[4]

Muhammad and the Jews: Round Two in Medina

"Can't we all just get along?" Within one year of moving to Medina, Muhammad answered that question with a resounding "No!" Upon changing locations, Muhammad had decided to start with a message of inclusion. Why not try a peaceful, politically correct message of unity? That would be a great way to bring in the Jews. The "revelations" during this time had a kinder, gentler tone. And several stories from the Bible were included in the Koran, although most of them were misquoted or just flat wrong. Also, in many ways the various teachings in the Koran sounded like an Arabic version of Judaism. Muhammad advocated that his followers wash before prayer, fast, avoid pork, and adopt the law of retribution with its well-known "eye for an eye" command. Amazingly, Muslims were not instructed to pray toward Mecca during this time. Muhammad's hometown was not considered holy in the least after his quick deportation. No, during the first year in Medina the follower of Muhammad was commanded to pray toward the holy city of Jerusalem. Can you imagine what would happen to a Muslim if he did that today?

In his excellent work *Islam and the Jews: The Unfinished Battle*, Mark Gabriel lists the five most important Koranic declarations concerning the Jews that were written during these early years:

---

4. Mark Gabriel, *Islam and the Jews: The Unfinished Battle* (Lake Mary, FL: Charisma House, 2003), 111.

1. The Jews are Allah's only chosen people. Sura 2:47
2. Allah protected the Jews when they were living as strangers in a foreign land. Sura 28:4–6
3. Allah chose all of his prophets from the Jewish people. Sura 5:20
4. Allah would be kind to Jews (and Christians) who believed in one God and performed good works. Sura 2:62 and Sura 5:69
5. Allah would bless the Jews (and Christians) who practiced the teachings of their holy books. Sura 5:44, 46–47[5]

Not only was the new religion accommodating to the Jews of Medina, but in some cases it actually put them on a pedestal. Muhammad wanted to make Islam attractive to the Jews. And why not? Mark Gabriel tells us there were three major Jewish tribes living in Medina.[6] Certainly this message would resonate with the Jews. But the strategy failed to work. Round Two in Medina turned out to be worse than Round One in Mecca. Muhammad passionately wanted the Jewish people to validate his status as a prophet. But in the end there were too many barriers for them to hurdle in order to join the new religion.

If the Mecca strategy was a failure, then the Medina strategy was an all-out catastrophe. But why? Why was Muhammad striking out with the Jews?

- The problem could have been racial. Were the Jews

---

5. Ibid., 73–76.
6. Ibid., 107.

unable to stomach being told what to do by someone from Arab rather than Jewish stock?

- Perhaps it was because Muhammad was illiterate and uneducated. Did the Jews think he was just some kind of hick from the desert who had spent too many years outside in the sun?

- Maybe Muhammad didn't have adequate social standing for the Jews. If he had been more of a mover and shaker, would they have accepted him?

The answer to all of these questions, of course, is no. If the barrier was purely racial, as a result of the Jews feeling superior to the Arabs, then why did they choose to live with them in the first place? They were surrounded by Arabs in Arabia: so if they harbored intense prejudice, surely they would have just moved.

If a lack of education turned the Jews off to Muhammad, then they would have had to throw out much of the Old Testament. David, the most loved king in Israel's history, wrote many of the psalms, but his educational background consisted of shepherding sheep in the pastures of Bethlehem. Amos, a great prophet of God, was also a shepherd with no educational background. There were many others. Certainly Jews have been among the most educated people on the face of the earth. They value learning. But many of their heroes never cracked a book.

Was the problem merely Muhammad's social standing? Again, the answer is no. Until he was forty years old, Muhammad was known in the region as a businessman. That was right up the

Jews' alley. They excelled in business, and no doubt many of them had dealt with Muhammad on previous occasions.

The Jews had no ulterior motives as far as Islam goes. Their decision was an objective one made by observing the evidence. Why Muhammad was rejected was plain and simple. It had to do with the shortcomings of the Prophet himself.

Ibn Ishaq began carefully cataloging the biography of Muhammad about a century after Muhammad's death. Although that work has been lost, another faithful follower of Muhammad, Ibn Hisham, edited it and left behind two comprehensive works on the life of Muhammad. In 834 the abridged and condensed work appeared, and it is a gold mine for understanding Islam and its origins. The following quote is from this work. Two of Muhammad's followers went to talk to the Jewish rabbis of Medina to find out what they thought about the messages and the man behind them.

> They were there to tell them about Muhammad, his sayings, and his behavior, and ask them what they thought about him, since the rabbis belonged to the People of the Book, had knowledge of the ancient Scriptures and of the Prophets, which they themselves knew nothing about. They traveled to Medina and sought out the rabbis. There they spoke to them about Muhammad. Their answer was: "Ask him three questions that we give you. If he answers them, he is an anointed prophet; if not, then he is a liar. Be careful how you act towards him.

Ask him what happened to the men who vanished in ancient times, for they have a wonderful story. Ask him also about the traveler who reached the outer limits of East and West. Ask him about the spirit as well. If he answers you, follow him, for he is a prophet. If he says nothing, he is a liar." Then they went to Muhammad and asked him the three questions. Muhammad responded with assurance. "Tomorrow I will have an answer for you." But he waited fifteen nights without receiving a revelation. So they gathered and said, "Now fifteen nights have already passed." Muhammad himself was very disturbed that no revelation was given.[7]

Muhammad finally received a visit from "Gabriel," but Muhammad never answered the three questions. Strike one.

Another basis for the Jews' rejection of Muhammad came from his supposed "holy book." It just didn't line up with the Jewish Scriptures. Not even close! It seemed like nonsense to them, and they had no problem telling him so. Prosperous Jews lived in sections of Medina. Some of the Jews in Medina were respected rabbis, well known as scholars of the Torah. They knew the Old Testament inside and out. In fact, before Israel became a nation in 1948, some of the most observant Jewish communities survived and even bloomed in the Arab Middle East. Muhammad recounted the story of Moses, Pharaoh, and the exodus in the Koran. He must have liked the story, because he told it twenty-seven times! Yet the central message of the exodus is missing.

---

7. Ibn Hisham, *The Life of Muhammad, Volume 1: The Persecuted Prophet in Mecca* (Villach, Austria: Light of Life Publishing, 1997), 103.

The Passover is not mentioned even once. And the Koran was supposed to go over with the Jews? Nonetheless, Muhammad's followers earnestly wanted to see how their new leader stacked up to Abraham, Moses, and the other prophets of Judaism. So Muhammad's "prophecies" were scrutinized by the Jewish think tank of the day. And the result was strike two.

Were the Arabs Left Out in the Cold?

The Jews had the Torah and the Christians had the Bible, but the Arabs had nothing. In his book *Envy: The Enemy Within*, Bob Sorge illuminates the situation with these words: "There is good reason to connect the current tensions in the Middle East with the envy-induced parting of ways that happened between Isaac and Ishmael almost 4,000 years ago. Because he envied the favor granted to his brother, Ishmael mocked Isaac and was cast out of the house by Isaac's mother, Sarah. The ripple effect of the envy between those two brothers is still being felt today through the various descendants, most specifically in today's Israeli-Arab conflicts."[8]

Was the problem a matter of age-old envy between the cousins of the Middle East? Did the Arabs think they were playing second fiddle to the Jews again? Some historians believe the Christians of the day seemed to be more content to poke fun at the Arabs and ridicule them rather than to attempt to convert them to faith in Jesus. Karen Armstrong picks this thought up and gives it support:

---

8. Bob Sorge, *Envy: The Enemy Within* (Ventura, CA: Regal Books, 2003), 13.

There was also spiritual restlessness in Mecca and throughout the peninsula. Arabs knew that Judaism and Christianity, which were practiced in the Byzantine and Persian empires, were more sophisticated than their own pagan traditions. Some had come to believe that the High God of their pantheon, al-Lah (whose name simply meant "the God"), was the deity worshiped by Jews and the Christians, but he had sent the Arabs no prophet and no scripture in their own language. Indeed, the Jews and Christians whom they met often taunted the Arabs for being left out of the divine plan. Throughout Arabia one tribe fought another, in a murderous cycle of vendetta and counter-vendetta. It seemed to many of the more thoughtful people in Arabia that the Arabs were a lost people, exiled forever from the civilized world and ignored by God himself.[9]

So how did we get from a strong Arab Christian church to the place where Islam has virtually swallowed up Arab culture completely? The answer is simple. Force people to convert. Since Muhammad could not offer one miracle as evidence to back up his claim to be a prophet, other tactics would need to be used. The deciding conversion factor had little to do with beliefs. The Koran was written with clear orders to Muhammad's followers on how to convert people.

One out of every fifty-five verses in the Koran is a verse on war. There are 109 verses in all that are identified as war verses.

9. Karen Armstrong, *Islam: A Short History* (New York: Modern Library, 2000), 3.

In his timely book *Secrets of the Koran*, Don Richardson writes, "War verses are scattered throughout Mohammad's chapters like blood splattered at a crime scene."[10] Richardson goes on:

> Troops of modern Muslim apologists, whitewash and brush in hand, strain their brains trying to justify the original mini-genocide that Mohammed was about to unleash on the Jews in Medina. They also try to disconnect his murders there from the numerous copycat atrocities that his followers, honoring his example, were to perpetrate down through the subsequent centuries of Islamic history. I call them modern Muslim apologists because during most of the 1,400 years since Mohammad's time Muslims have enjoyed such total control in North Africa and the Middle East that few people have ever dared ask them to justify anything. Times are different now, and Muslims are trying to develop apologetic skills. But they have yet to encounter the full weight of critical investigation of which free Western minds are capable. In other words, the ground has just begun to heat up under Islam's feet.[11]

Muhammad did not bring peace anywhere he went. He killed at will, threatened entire villages, and used some of the most gruesome torture methods known to humankind. Richardson provides a complete list of the 109 verses on war.

10. Don Richardson, *Secrets of the Koran: Revealing Insights into Islam's Holy Book* (Ventura, CA: Regal Books, 2003), 28.
11. Ibid., 33.

Here are some of the Koranic verses that Muslim scholars have trouble explaining.

> "Strike off their heads. Strike off their finger-tips . . . because they defied God and his Apostle." Sura 8:12–13

> "Seize them and put them to death wherever you find them." Sura 4:89

> "Believers, make war on the infidels who dwell around you." Sura 9:123

> "When you meet the unbelievers in the battlefield strike off their heads and, when you have laid them low, bind your captives firmly." Sura 47:4[12]

There is no way around it: Muhammad practiced violence and called his followers to do the same. Yet Arab culture, in which Islam was birthed, has so many positives. Arab hospitality is considered to be among the best in the world. My wife, JoAnn, and I have experienced it firsthand on several occasions. The Arabs' humble desert beginnings allow them to be accepting and kind to strangers. They are warm and friendly; and once you eat a meal in their home, you are family. The Arabs would have flourished as Christians! And in fact the church is thriving in Arab countries today, even in the midst of harsh treatment from Islam.

Did the church miss a golden opportunity with the Arabs? A casual glance at church history tells us that this contention is

---

12. Ibid., 55, 58.

false. The church did not fail when it came to reaching out to Arabs.

We see in Acts 2 that the New Testament church was born on the day of Pentecost when the Holy Spirit descended on an ethnically diverse group assembled in Jerusalem. Arabs were there, and they heard the believers declare the wonders of God in the Arabic language. God miraculously gave Jesus' followers the ability to bring the message to each group in its native tongue. The Arabs were in no way left out as they witnessed the phenomenon. They heard Peter's sermon, given in the universally spoken Greek language. And the message was clear: Salvation is for all people. About three thousand people responded with repentance and were baptized that day. Arabs were involved in the church from day one.

The first Christian ruler in history was in fact an Arab. Abgar VIII, also known as Abgar the Great, converted to Christianity around the year AD 200 and lived in Edessa, which is in present-day Turkey. Although Turkey is a non-Arab country, Abgar was an Arab living in what was then an Assyrian country. Also, the Nabateans of southern Jordan and northern Arabia converted to Christianity in mass and developed a vibrant church in the region. The Nabateans are best known for their amazing city carved out of the slope of Mount Hor where Aaron the brother of Moses is buried. Petra of Indiana Jones fame is the famous city they built. In Petra's heyday, the population exceeded twenty thousand. Also, the Ghassanids, a group of Arabian tribes that migrated from Yemen to southern Syria, converted to Christianity. They became a force in the Byzantine church and resisted Islam as it swept through Syria a few centuries later.[13]

Kenneth Cragg, in his book *The Arab Christian: A History in the Middle East*, supports the idea that Arabs were a major part of the early church. He writes, "There are aspects of being Arab that almost necessitate its equation with Islam. That fact has been the burden of Arab Christianity since the seventh Christian century. Yet Christian faith had a long history within Arabia in the six centuries before Islam emerged to dominate the ethnic and cultural determinants of Arab existence."[14]

I believe God is currently bringing the Arab people back to the great days they enjoyed as an essential part of Christ's church. The tide has turned; there is a new day in the Middle East. Muslims are coming to Jesus, and the church is blessed to have them. To Muslims who read this book, we want you to know that we love you. And I pray that this book touches your heart.

---

13. Kenneth Cragg, *The Arab Christian: A History in the Middle East* (Louisville: John Knox Press, 1991), 13.
14. Ibid.

Fundamental Beliefs Of Islam

1 God (Allah)

The Arabic word for God, meaning simply "the one to be worshiped and obeyed." (Like Elohim in Hebrew)

2 Angels

God's servants (messengers) in heaven. Gabriel is the Angel of Revelation who Muslims believe recited the Qur'an to Mohammed.

3 Books (Scriptures)

The Qur'an but also scriptures that were revealed before it, especially the Torah, Psalms, and the Gospel.

4 Prophets

Mohammed, "the seal of the prophets," but also the prophets who came before him, especially Adam, Noah, Abraham, Moses, and Jesus.

5 Day of Judgement

Allah will judge mankind by their deeds. All will enter either Paradise (the Garden) or Hell (the Fire).

Used by permission.

4

The Power of Love

*You have heard that it was said, "Love your
neighbor and hate your enemy." But I tell you:
Love your enemies and pray for those who
persecute you, that you may be sons of your
Father in heaven.*

Jesus speaking in Matthew 5:43–45

The collision of history, religion, and politics make the
Middle East terribly volatile. But toss into the mix advanced
weapons (in the last few years the arms race in the Middle East
has been growing at an alarming rate), and the whole world
becomes unstable. Yes, there is a war going on in Iraq and in
Afghanistan. But I'm talking about a regional war that could
involve multiple nations in the Middle East. And I believe that
kind of war could escalate quickly, with nations like Russia,

North Korea, the United States, and possibly even China getting involved.

Prospects for peace in the Middle East currently appear to be at an all-time low. A steady stream of headlines from the region continues to fuel global anxiety about a major war on the horizon. As I write this today, here are just a few of the headlines from the region:

> *Iran Could Have Nukes This Year*
>
> *Gaza Rockets Fall during Holocaust Ceremony in Israel*
>
> *Israel Air Strike on Syria Sent a Strong Message*
>
> *Syria Won't Cut Iran, Hezbollah Ties in Peace Deal*[1]

At the center of the storm is Israel. Surrounding nations pose a threat to the nation's very existence. Iran's president, Mahmoud Ahmadinejad, has threatened to annihilate the Jewish state. Islamic fundamentalists picture a future Middle East minus Israel altogether. The Israelis continue to arm themselves with the latest weapons, and the Islamic nations that surround them are not far behind.

There is one weapon being used in the Middle East today, however, that has more power than any weapon of mass destruction ever invented—and the results speak for themselves. That weapon is love.

I know this may sound corny or trite. But I'm not talking about some kind of sappy, sentimental love that you hear about

---

1. *Israel Today* magazine, http://www.israeltoday.co.il/, May 1, 2008.

in a love song. The people who have this kind of love are willing to risk their lives to share it. And they even share it with their enemies.

A Jew, a Palestinian, and a Border Crossing

Aaron is a messianic Jew who doesn't have a hateful bone in his body. He used to have plenty of bitterness, but Jesus delivered him from it all.

While serving in the Israeli army and encountering numerous conflicts with Palestinians, Aaron saw things that were hard to forget. He dealt with his pain by burying those memories deep inside. Close friends were killed in suicide bombings that specifically targeted Israeli soldiers. Hezbollah terrorists used women and children as human shields in Lebanon. Shoot-outs with Hamas in the Gaza Strip were some of the worst experiences of his life. All of this contributed to Aaron's hate for Arabs, Muslims in particular. Aaron would be the first to say that Israel didn't do everything right, either. That bothered him too, since he was a part of it. He didn't sleep well.

Miraculously Aaron opened his heart to Jesus as his Savior a few years after his military service. Over time he was also released from the anger that had controlled him. An Arabic pastor preached one Saturday in the messianic congregation that Aaron attended. Aaron cried throughout the sermon, as God began to replace his hatred for Arabs with love.

Aaron became friends with Palestinian believers in the West Bank, in places like Ramallah and Bethlehem, and began to visit them. Since he didn't look Jewish, he was able to move around in Palestinian areas with ease. They studied the Bible and prayed together; but since many of these believers had come from a Muslim background, Aaron was careful as he met with them. He developed a love for his new friends and soon realized what it was like to live on the other side of the fence between Israel and the Palestinian territories. Some of Aaron's Jewish friends who weren't Christians told him that he had lost his mind. To them he was becoming friends with the enemy.

Aaron's friends weren't the only ones who thought he had lost his mind. Suspicious Palestinian guards often questioned him on his way in or out of the West Bank. On one occasion he was interrogated and accused of being an Israeli spy.

One day their suspicion turned to violence. Israel had just completed a military campaign in Jenin, so the West Bank was tense. Aaron had stayed out of Ramallah during the conflict, but he felt that things had settled down. Hamdi was one of the Palestinian guards that day at the border crossing only a few miles from Jerusalem. He was a committed Muslim and had been in several battles with the Israel Defense Forces. As Aaron got in line, Hamdi questioned him about why he was in the West Bank. Fearing that if he was too specific some of the Palestinian believers might be compromised and eventually persecuted, Aaron kept his answers short and somewhat evasive.

Aaron certainly knew how to defend himself, but he had decided in advance that if he was ever attacked for being a believer he wouldn't fight back. Since Jesus didn't fight back when he was questioned and beaten before his crucifixion, neither would he.

Getting nowhere with his questioning, Hamdi, out of frustration, slapped Aaron's face. With no Israeli guards in sight and the Israeli military out of the West Bank, Hamdi realized he had the chance for which he had long been waiting. He would beat the Jew until he begged for mercy. And beat him he did. Hamdi enjoyed it for a while; but when Aaron took every punch in silence, Hamdi's determination to make a fool of him faded. Aaron lay on the cement, covered in blood.

But then it happened. Hamdi says he learned a lesson that would change the entire trajectory of his life. Aaron slowly arose and looked Hamdi directly in the eyes. Then, in all sincerity, he said, "I am sorry that I made you angry. I pray that you will forgive me. I know things are probably tough here in the West Bank for you and your family. I am going to pray to Jesus for you. I know that you hate me, but Jesus said to love our enemies."

With those words Aaron leaned forward and gave Hamdi a hug. Then he was on his way.

As Hamdi was telling me this story just a few months ago, he said this was the most powerful moment of his life. "I could not forget those words. They replayed in my ears over and over for the next few days. I realized that the people of my religion have plenty of weapons. We've had the best swords for 1,400 years now! We have plenty of hate that makes us want to kill anyone who gets in our way. But we don't have love. How could a Jew take that kind of beating from me and then turn around and show love to me? I had to find out."

Hamdi went on a quest, and God led him straight to some new believers in the West Bank. They answered all of his questions, and the power of the Holy Spirit pierced his heart. He got on his knees and gave his life to Jesus.

Hamdi grew in his faith rapidly. He accepted Jesus' love and forgiveness about ten years ago, and he now pastors a church somewhere in the West Bank. The turnaround has been miraculous.

"Islam is cracking from the inside," Hamdi says. "They thought that all Christians hated them, just as I did. But now they are seeing love. It's our job to bring it to them. It took a Jew to show me how God's love operates. He should have hated me for all I did to him, but he loved me. God has now sent me to bring this message to Palestinians who need to know about the love of Jesus. When a believer has the Word of God and the love of God in his heart, this is irresistible."

Why Muslims Love Jesus and Follow Him

J. Dudley Woodberry is professor of Islamic studies at the School of Intercultural Studies at Fuller Theological Seminary in Pasadena, California. He also lived in the Muslim world for many years. In the October 2007 issue of *Christianity Today*, Woodberry shared the results of a survey of converts from the religion of Islam. He stated that the survey doesn't claim scientific precision but rather offers a glimpse of how the Holy Spirit is attracting Muslims to Jesus Christ.

From 1991 to 2007 about 750 Muslims who had converted to Christianity filled out an extensive survey about why they chose to follow Jesus. Those who responded were from thirty countries and fifty different ethnic groups. Despite the diversity, trends developed that were consistent regardless of the respondent's ethnicity or country of origin. Here are five of the key influences that God used to bring these former Muslims to Christ:

- the lifestyle of Christians
- the power of God in answered prayers and healing
- dissatisfaction with the type of Islam they had experienced
- the spiritual truth in the Bible
- the love expressed through the life and teachings of Jesus

Ranking "the lifestyle of Christians" as the greatest factor in their decision to follow Christ, many of the respondents were particularly attracted to the way they saw Christians treat others with love. An Egyptian, for instance, appreciated the love of a Christian group at a university in the United States, whereas he experienced unloving attitudes from Muslim students and faculty at a university in Saudi Arabia. Others were impressed by the love they observed in Christian marriages.[2]

JoAnn and I often hear similar comments from our Muslim friends in the Middle East. They tell us that they find Christians to be loving and compassionate people. They have been surprised at how they, as Muslims, have been loved by Christians; and this leaves quite an impression on them.

2. J. Dudley Woodberry, Russell G. Shubin, and G. Marks, "Why Muslims Follow Jesus: The Results of a Recent Survey of Converts from Islam," *Christianity Today*, October 2007, http://www.christianitytoday.com/ct/2007/october/42.80.html?start=1.

Such love, of course, is directly related to Jesus Christ living in us. He is the author of love. We are simply following him and his teaching to love others. But did you know that the Koran recognizes this as well? Woodberry writes, "The Qur'an already calls [Jesus] faultless (19:19). Many Muslims are attracted to him by his description in the Qur'an and then go to the Gospels to find out more." One Muslim man was moved by the depiction of Jesus as the Good Shepherd. Another was touched by the love shown in a tender scene portrayed in a Christmas Eve service.[3]

We shouldn't be surprised that love is the magnet that attracts the people of Islam. This is the message that sets Christianity apart. Perhaps you've heard it said that "Christianity isn't a religion—it's a relationship with God." How true. And who doesn't want a relationship with God?

Some people think they have a relationship with God only to find out that they really don't. Usually this discovery occurs in the midst of a trial. A woman in Iran experienced this a few years ago. God used her difficult circumstances to show her that she needed him more than anyone or anything else. It's hard to live in Iran. It's *really hard* to live in Iran if you're Jewish.

A Jewish Woman, a Muslim Man, and the Ayatollah

In 1979 the Iranian Revolution, also known as the Islamic Revolution, swept through Iran like a tsunami. In a matter of days the government of the nation went from progressive to

---

3. Ibid.

repressive. It was out with the new and in with the old. The shah of Iran loved the West and was a progressive leader. But once he was deposed, the nation of Iran had a rude awakening: Sharia law. The people found themselves controlled by one new rule after another. The Iranians we have talked to who were there at the time have all said that it was the ultimate nightmare.

Can you imagine living in Iran and realizing that everything had changed almost overnight? The revolution was an attempt to return to a form of "literal Islam." But what if you lived there and you were not a Muslim? What if you lived there and you were Jewish?

Are you surprised to hear of Jews living in Iran? Jews actually have lived in Iran for over 2,700 years. When the northern kingdom of Israel fell in 722 BC, some Israelites were exiled among the towns of the Medes in modern-day Iran (see 2 Kings 17:6). After the destruction of Jerusalem in 586 BC, the kingdom of Judah was taken into captivity in Babylon, present-day Iraq. Then, following the Persians' conquest of Babylon in 539 BC, some Jews evidently moved eastward into the cities of Medo-Persia. Around 460 BC the Jewish maiden Esther, or Hadassah in Hebrew, became the queen when she married King Xerxes. Jews have continued to live there ever since.

But when strict Islam came to have firm control, Iran was no longer the country it once was. For centuries Iranian Jews had gotten along just fine in the home of the old Persian Empire. But then Ayatollah Khomeini began to routinely voice his disgust for the nation of Israel. Israel was now "the little Satan," and America was "the great Satan." Jews generally had been accepted in Iran and free to practice Judaism. This new focus on Israel as the enemy of Iran, which began in 1979, convinced some to migrate back to the land of their ancestors. In 1948 the Jewish population in Iran was about 100,000. On the eve of the Islamic Revolution in 1979, 80,000 Jews lived there. The Jewish Virtual Library claims that the Jewish community in Iran is one of the oldest Jewish communities outside Israel—representing, with a population of approximately 25,000, the second-largest Jewish community, after Israel, in the Middle East.[4]

Shireen and her family were Jews, but they loved Iran and decided to stay. Privately they hoped the ayatollah and his regime would be overthrown one day and things would get back to normal. But even though Shireen felt guilty for feeling this way about her heritage, Judaism for her had become stale, predictable, and unfulfilling.

Shireen realized that questioning Judaism openly would bring unbearable pain to her family. After all, her ancestors had survived some twenty-seven centuries outside of Israel and kept the faith through intermittent oppression and persecution. Nevertheless, she was empty. She had never considered converting to Islam, even though some of her relatives had done so under pressure. Shireen detested having to dress like a Muslim in public. Since the revolution, the government instituted mandatory Islamic dress for every woman—even visitors. Grudgingly she put on a chador and scarf each day as she headed out to work.

---

4. "The Jews of Iran," Jewish Virtual Library, http://www.jewishvirtuallibrary. org/jsource/anti-semitism/iranjews.html#1.

Shireen's bank position paid the bills, and she hoped to get married some day and raise a family. Hassan worked in the same bank. Shireen admired him because he treated her with respect and was so pleasant to everyone. The mood always changed when Hassan walked into the room. One day both of them were eating lunch in the breakroom, and the room suddenly became empty. Shireen decided to ask Hassan a question. "How do you do it, Hassan? You always have a smile on your face. I don't get it."

Hassan looked around, took a deep breath, and said: "Shireen, I am a follower of Jesus. He has changed everything about me. I didn't used to be this way."

Shireen was shocked. "I can't believe you said that. You could get killed for talking like that. What if the Islamic clerics or the ayatollah himself heard this?" Then she asked, "But you were a Muslim, and now you really are a follower of Jesus?"

"Yes I am!" Hassan blurted out with a big smile.

Shireen questioned him further: "Why would you switch religions? What's the difference?"

Hassan took advantage of this opportunity to explain his faith in Jesus Christ, which he did beautifully. He ended by saying, "It's religion that you are sick of, Shireen. And so was I. But now I have a relationship with a loving Father, and that was something that I could not have in Islam."

Shireen began to open up, saying, "But I am not a Muslim."

"I know that, Shireen," Hassan immediately responded. "You're Jewish, I can tell. Even though your ancestors have lived here for centuries and in many ways assimilated into the Persian culture, there are still differences between our races and religions. I have known that you are Jewish for a long time, and I have been praying for you every day!"

"With those words," Shireen recalls, "I knew Hassan's faith in Christ was what I had been desperately searching for and what had been missing in my life. Jesus had to be the answer to all my questions about God. Can you imagine how powerfully this hit me? *Here was a Muslim man telling me—a Jewish woman—about Jesus. We live in Iran! Talk about risk!* Hassan's love for Jesus was all over his face. And Jesus put that love in his heart for *me*. He prayed for me, and his passion for communicating the truth to me transcended any fear he might have of getting caught."

Shireen received Christ in the breakroom of the bank that day. "I was forgiven, and I had a relationship with my loving Father in heaven, who had pursued me."

Later that week Shireen left her apartment at midnight and traveled a few miles to an address that Hassan had given her. She knew it was dangerous, but she wanted to attend her first Christian worship service—an underground meeting in a home. The believers, all of them former Muslims like Hassan, were waiting for her. When Shireen walked into the basement of the house, they jumped to their feet with applause and hugged her so hard that she thought she would be crushed!

These believers worshiped and praised the Lord with all of their hearts. The leader of the group then shared how Hassan had told them about the burden he had felt for Shireen to find

Christ. "So we have been praying for you for months now, Shireen. Welcome to Jesus' family!"

Today Shireen is involved in ministry. She is also married. No, she didn't marry Hassan! She married a wonderful man who grew up a Muslim and came to Christ about the same time that Shireen did. Considering the world in which we live today, I am amazed that a Jewish woman married an Iranian Muslim man. Only God could pull that one off! Shireen and her husband are now serving their Savior in Europe. Hassan has also gotten married, and he still lives in Iran.

As Shireen told me her story, I took notes as fast as I could. All the while I was wiping away tears, as was she. Shireen closed with these words that I will never forget: "Tom, none of the world's problems will ever be solved through politics. None of them will be solved through war, either. When you give your life to Jesus, he fills you with his love. All of the barriers between races and religions become meaningless. He is the only one who can break through all of that. Hassan could be in jail for telling me about Jesus, but he didn't care. It was worth it to him. And when I walked into that room and thirty former Muslims were jumping up and down, hugging and loving this little Jewish girl, then I knew that I truly had found God."

Hamsa—Former Tank Driver for Saddam Hussein Finds Jesus

Hamsa was an Iraqi through and through. He loved his country and couldn't imagine living anywhere else. As a young boy he admired Saddam Hussein—who was going to be the great liberator of the Muslims—and made a commitment to serve him till death.

Saddam believed he was the successor of Nebuchadnezzar, the renowned Babylonian king who conquered Jerusalem and took the Israelites into captivity in 586 BC.[5] So did Hamsa. He had seen the pictures throughout Baghdad that portrayed Nebuchadnezzar as his face morphed into Saddam's likeness. Saddam was the great Arabic hero. Surely he would be the leader who would bring Muslims back together. One day they were going to rule the world for the glory of Allah.

The first Gulf War began, and Hamsa could hardly believe he had attained the high privilege of driving a tank for the great Saddam Hussein. They would certainly defeat the Americans and establish Iraq as the new Islamic leader in the Middle East. During the first few months of the war, however, Hamsa saw things he thought he would never see in his whole life. Iraqi soldiers were surrendering in record numbers to the Americans.

How could this be? Hamsa wondered. *We are going to prevail. Islam cannot be defeated. Why are they surrendering?*

About that time Hamsa's best friend, Abdul, began to talk to him about some kind of spiritual experience he had encountered. If there was ever a committed Muslim, it was Abdul—or so Hamsa believed. Hamsa thought Abdul's religious experience was weird, since it involved Jesus. *What's this all about?* he wondered. *What does Jesus have to do with anything?*

---

5. Charles H. Dyer, *The Rise of Babylon: Sign of the End Times* (Wheaton: Tyndale, 1991), 41.

Jesus had a lot to do with Abdul's life, and soon he would have a lot to do with Hamsa's life. For two years Abdul shared Jesus with Hamsa. They had been best friends since going to grade school together in Baghdad, so Hamsa listened to Abdul out of respect. But he wasn't interested—until he had a dream about Jesus himself. Jesus was on the other side of a lake, and he called for Hamsa to come and follow him. "Forsake Allah and follow me!" Hamsa couldn't believe what was happening to him. After the dream, all he could think about was Jesus.

Hamsa said to Abdul, "I would believe in Jesus, but the Bible is corrupted. I don't believe it is true."

"Really?" Abdul responded. "Have you ever read it? I do have a copy of the Bible."

Hamsa couldn't resist the challenge. He gladly took the Bible from Abdul because he was so excited to prove that his friend was wrong. But Hamsa turned out to be the one who was wrong!

"All I know is that when I began reading the New Testament I fell in love with Jesus," Hamsa recalls. "I couldn't believe how compassionately he dealt with people. In John, chapter four, a woman came to him, and he was so gentle with her—but straightforward. In Islam, she would have been a dead woman. She was immoral, but Jesus treated her like a human being. I had never seen this in my religion."

Hamsa thought to himself, *OK, the New Testament is acceptable; but the Old Testament was written by the Jews, and they are sneaky. I'm sure they have changed it for their benefit. They must have corrupted it.*

"But after reading the Old Testament, I learned something about the Jews," Hamsa states. "They didn't write the Old Testament on their own. God had to have written the Old Testament. There was no other explanation for it. If the Jews had written the Old Testament by themselves, they certainly would have made themselves look a whole lot better! The Old Testament showed that the Jews were human. They made mistakes—a lot of mistakes. I could find no fault in the Old Testament, either."

Hamsa had a big problem. How could he be anything other than a Muslim? That was the faith of his father and his family. He was so confused. He loved Jesus, and he had read the entire Bible and believed it was the truth. What about Muhammad and the Koran? Hamsa had heard the gospel from his friend Abdul for two years now. He had read the New Testament. Then he had also read the Old Testament. On top of that he had a vivid dream about Jesus calling him to follow him. But he was a Muslim. What was he supposed to do?

Hamsa decided to ask Jesus to give him proof. He came to the conclusion that he should fast and pray for thirty days. He pleaded with God to reveal himself. Being a Muslim, if he came to the conclusion that Jesus, not Allah, was Lord, his life would be altered forever.

It was January 2000. For thirty days Hamsa prayed and fasted, pleading with God for an answer. Jesus was moving in his heart, and on day thirty he had a breakthrough. Jesus appeared to Hamsa again in a vision. And again Jesus was calling him to salvation: "Forsake Allah and come to me."

Hamsa was convinced. Although it was the middle of the night, he called Abdul, who rushed to Hamsa's home. That night Hamsa prayed to receive Jesus as his Savior.

His whole life changed. Hamsa knew he needed to get away. He and Abdul left Iraq later that week and went to Jordan. There Hamsa met many believers and grew rapidly in his faith. Then, after living in Amman for a few years, he knew it was time to go back to Iraq and make a difference in his war-torn country.

Today Hamsa is a pastor in Baghdad. He shares the gospel virtually every day with Iraqis who are frustrated with Islam and are desperate to find God. Hamsa intends to never leave his country again. He is willing to die for Jesus in Iraq.

He may have to. Hamsa's assistant pastor lost his life for Jesus this year. Like Hamsa, Khalid came to Christ from a Muslim background. He was kidnapped and told that if he didn't reject Jesus he would be killed. Khalid told his Muslim abductors that Jesus had given him peace in life and that he was sure Jesus would give him peace in death. The kidnappers slit Khalid's throat and left him to die in the street. He is a martyr for Jesus.

Hamsa lives in Baghdad under constant threats. But he will not give up. "How can I leave the people I love when Jesus has chosen me to bring them his words of life?"

Hamsa is God's man in Baghdad.

*He has rescued us from the dominion of
darkness and brought us into the kingdom*

of the Son he loves, in whom we have
redemption, the forgiveness of sins.

Colossians 1:13

The Power of Forgiveness

You have heard that it was said, "Eye for eye, and tooth for tooth." But I tell you, Do not resist an evil person. If someone strikes you on the right cheek, turn to him the other also.

Jesus speaking in Matthew 5:38–39

Unfortunately, there was a time when we Christians weren't known in the Muslim world for our love. We were known, rather, for our hate. This time period—the time period of the Crusades—surely constitutes one of the darkest chapters of church history.

When you hear the word *crusader* or *crusade*, what do you think of? Christians have mixed feelings. On the one hand, the Billy Graham crusades have seen millions of people come to Christ worldwide through the preaching of one of the greatest evangelists of all time. But on the other hand, many Christian high schools throughout America have named their sports teams the Crusaders and have reaped much criticism for it.

When President Bush gave his speech to the American people one week after 9/11, he stated that America was going on a "crusade against terrorism." Peter Ford, from the *Christian Science Monitor*, wrote, "President Bush's reference to a 'crusade' against terrorism, which passed almost unnoticed by Americans, rang alarm bells in Europe. It raised fears that the terrorist attacks could spark a 'clash of civilizations' between Christians and Muslims, sowing fresh winds of hatred and mistrust."[1]

The Muslim world protested the very use of this word *crusade*. So what is all the anxiety about? For the answer to that question we have to go back about nine centuries and travel to Europe.

In the year 1095 Pope Urban II spoke at a gathering of about three hundred Catholic clerics from throughout France. After nine days of meetings, it was time for the pope to give a speech. This was not just any speech, as history would later prove. The pope spoke passionately regarding the need for the Latin church to defend its fellow Greek Christians who had been invaded by the Turkish Muslims. The capital city of the Eastern church was Constantinople. The capital city of the Western church was Rome. In 1054 the church had split in two during a dispute over papal authority. The Great Schism divided the church, and

---

1. Peter Ford, "Europe Cringes at Bush 'Crusade' against Terrorists," *Christian Science Monitor*, September 19, 2001, http://www.csmonitor. com/2001/0919/p12s2-woeu.html.

it was now weaker as a result. With the Greek church based in Constantinople and the Latin church based in Rome, the strategic advances of Islam became all the more dangerous.

Urban called on the church to do two things: (1) liberate the Eastern church from Islamic advances into the region, and (2) liberate Jerusalem, and specifically the Church of the Holy Sepulchre, from Muslim domination. At the end of the call to action, the audience began to shout, "God wills it! God wills it!" To the pope's surprise, people rushed to the front of the auditorium and threw themselves at his feet, volunteering for service in the army of God. A revolution had begun.

Next the pope took his message on the road, and in a few months the ranks were swelling. From France to Germany, dukes, knights, the poor, convicts, bishops, and priests enlisted; and soon the soldiers were ready to make the trek of about two thousand miles to Jerusalem.[2]

The pope may have had an ulterior motive. He most definitely was interested in reuniting the Eastern and Western churches. If this happened, Urban's leadership would have been strengthened, and he would have established himself as God's leader to heal the split between the churches and bring them back together.

The pope used his papal authority to issue an edict that served as a great incentive to join the crusaders:

> I say to those who are present. I command that it
> be said to those who are absent. Christ commands it.

---

2. Justo L. Gonzalez, *The Story of Christianity, Volume 1: The Early Church to the Dawn of the Reformation* (New York: HarperCollins, 1984), 292.

> All who go thither and lose their lives, be it on the road
> or on the sea, or in the fight against the pagans, will
> be granted immediate forgiveness for their sins. This I
> grant to all who march, by virtue of the great gift which
> God has given me.
>
> —Pope Urban II[3]

With a clear mission to save Jerusalem, help the Eastern church, and be forgiven of sins, the offer was too good to refuse. The crusaders would get revenge on the Muslims who had destroyed the Church of the Holy Sepulchre in 1009 at the hands of Caliph al-Hakim of Egypt. After the caliph's death, the church was rebuilt; but the caliph had waged war on Christians and Jews with years of persecution. In 1005 al-Hakim ordered all Jews and Christians to wear belts around their necks in public to humiliate them. He finally expelled all Jews and Christians from Egypt.[4]

With vengeance in their hearts and a free pass when it came to sinning, the crusaders at times resembled barbarians. Like Islam, the church sought to expand its power with violence and forced conversions. Along their way the crusaders raped women, pillaged villages, and destroyed lives.

The Tafurs, a fringe group on the First Crusade, were filthy, barefoot peasants who would lead the charge into battle armed only with sticks. The Tafurs' fanaticism grew to a fever pitch, and

---

3. Ibid.
4. Elizabeth Hallam, ed., *Chronicles of the Crusades: Eye-witness Accounts of the Wars between Christianity and Islam* (New York: Welcome Rain, 2000), 24–25.

in Turkey they began to practice the unthinkable. Believing that Muslims were lower than animals, they began eating their victims. After promising a safe surrender to the people of Ma'arra, which is in present-day Syria, the Tafurs leveled the village and killed every inhabitant. They then put a dead man on a spit and roasted him like a pig. The Tafurs, unable to find any food, then proceeded to eat many of the people of the village. The Tafurs weren't the only crusaders who practiced cannibalism. The French army boasted about eating well on the bodies of the Saracens (a term used in the Middle Ages for those who practiced Islam).[5]

How sad that the name of Christ was connected to this debacle. As the crusaders traveled to fight the Holy War, the flags that led the troops boldly displayed the cross of Christ. The Crusades may have been spawned by some noble motives, but in the end they did amazing damage to the reputation of Christians in the Middle East. Since the peoples of the Middle East, especially Muslims, have memories that last for centuries, the Crusades are a major barrier to the evangelism of Muslims yet today. Even though the Crusades ended many centuries ago, Muslims remember them as if they occurred last week. Because they too suffered, Jews also have a negative view of this terrible period of Christian history.

Here are some interesting facts about the Crusades:

- Though history records four major crusades, there were actually hundreds of smaller crusades.
- The crusaders in the First Crusade overthrew the

---

5. Ibid., 85–86.

Muslims in Jerusalem, but they only held the Holy City for eighty-eight years.

- Women participated in the crusades, some even on the frontlines.

- Crusades were waged in almost every country in Europe and the Middle East.

- Several crusades were led by children, though none made it to the Holy Land.

- During the Fourth Crusade, Christians attacked Christians. The crusaders, from the Western church, intended to invade the Holy Land but got sidetracked and destroyed Constantinople, the great capital of the Eastern church.

- In the end, Muslims captured far more territory from Christians than vice versa.

- The Crusades were supported by such Christian saints as Bernard of Clairvaux, Catherine of Siena, Thomas Aquinas, and Francis of Assisi (though he did not fight).

- During the eleventh and twelfth centuries, crusading fervor broke out into savage persecutions of Jews. Some Christians slaughtered entire villages of Jews along the Rhine River.

- Crusades against Muslims continued in Spain and Portugal until 1492, when Isabella and Ferdinand ended them.

- In military terms, the Crusades to the Holy Land were an utter failure. Only the First Crusade accomplished the goal of capturing Jerusalem. This occurred on July 15, 1099.

- When the crusaders conquered Jerusalem, the new archbishop crowned one of the leaders, a French nobleman, as king. His title was Baldwin I of Jerusalem. He reigned for eighteen years before he died.[6]

By the conclusion of the Crusades, several things had become clear. Christianity is not the religion of the sword, and forced conversions are not our method of evangelism. Christians naturally view sites such as the Church of the Holy Sepulchre as important, but nowhere does Jesus call us to conquer lands in his name. The crusaders were completely out of control and disgraced the name of Jesus in the eyes of Muslims, Jews, and other Christians. The Muslims who fought them were also out of control, but they behaved no differently than had many Muslims for the previous five centuries. Muslims initiated hostilities years before Pope Urban II called for Christians to fight for Jerusalem.

For Muslims, the conclusion of the Crusades was an all-out victory. For believers, how we fought the Crusades is more important than the outcome. Fortunately, we have learned from this dark past. The Holy Spirit has more than enough power to convict the lost and produce conversions—even among Muslims in the Middle East. The Crusades showed a fundamental misunderstanding of how a person gets converted. It has little to do with us and everything to do with God's transforming power.

---

6. Caroline T. Marshall, "Did You Know? Little Known Facts about the Crusades," *Christian History & Biography*, October 1, 1993, 2.

And the Truth Will Set You Free

So what do we, as Christians, do with the Crusades? Just forget about them and move on? For those of us who work in the Islamic world, the Crusades are a major obstacle between us and Muslims. When I first heard that, I couldn't believe it. I knew that the church's behavior was reprehensible, but the Crusades in the Middle East ended over seven hundred years ago. America was at war with Japan less than seventy years ago, and today we consider them a strong ally. Neither side appears to harbor any animosity. But in the Middle East wounds heal slowly, if they heal at all.

When I'm talking with Muslims, I often bring up the Crusades as a point of conversation. I think it's best to hit the subject head-on and get the truth into the light. I tell them that Jesus never commanded us to convert people by force and to kill those who refuse. I admit that the church was wrong. If it seems appropriate, I even apologize to them—which is usually met with surprise.

In 1995 a group of Christians decided to bring a formal apology to Muslims, Jews, and Eastern Christians between Europe and the Middle East. About 150 people retraced the path of the First Crusade, starting at the cathedral of Cologne where it began exactly nine hundred years earlier. Their first stop was a Turkish mosque. Ergun and Emir Caner, in their excellent work titled *Christian Jihad*, retell the story.

> Their leader explained that the walkers had come to apologize for the atrocities committed in the name of Christ during the Crusades. Then they read a letter

of apology in German, Turkish, and English. They were "greeted with loud, sustained applause." The Imam responded: "When I heard the nature of your message, I was astonished and filled with hope. I thought to myself, 'whoever had this idea must have had an epiphany, a visit from God himself.' It is my wish that this project should become a very great success."[7]

Here is the statement that was read countless times throughout the journey:

Nine hundred years ago, our forefathers carried the name of Jesus Christ in battle across the Middle East. Fueled by fear, greed and hatred, they betrayed the name of Christ by conducting themselves in a manner contrary to his wishes and character. The Crusaders lifted the banner of the Cross above your people. By this act they corrupted its true meaning of reconciliation, forgiveness and selfless love.

On the anniversary of the First Crusade we also carry the name of Christ. We wish to retrace the footsteps of the Crusaders in apology for their deeds and in demonstration of the true meaning of the Cross. We deeply regret the atrocities committed in the name of Christ by our predecessors. We renounce greed, hatred and fear, and condemn all violence done in the name of Jesus Christ.

---

7. Ergun Mehmet Caner and Emir Fethi Caner, *Christian Jihad: Two Former Muslims Look at the Crusades and Killing in the Name of Christ* (Grand Rapids: Kregel Publications, 2004), 210–11.

Where they were motivated by hatred and prejudice, we offer love and brotherhood. Jesus the Messiah came to give life. Forgive us for allowing his name to be associated with death. Please accept again the true meaning of Messiah's words: "The Spirit of the Lord is upon me, because he has anointed me to bring the good news to the poor. He has sent me to proclaim release to the captives and recovery of sight to the blind, to let the oppressed go free, to proclaim the year of the Lord's favor."[8]

During my travels in the Middle East, I have met people who either heard this apology in person or heard about it from someone else. Thirteen years later I still come across people who talk about the group of Christians who came to say they were sorry. In the Middle East, where forgiveness is rare, we Christians could not carry with us a more powerful message.

Some Christians disagree with me. Paul Crawford takes an opposing opinion in an article in Christianity Today's *Christian History & Biography* magazine:

In the late 1990's, an American child led a "Reconciliation Walk" across Europe and the Middle East. . . . The child's activities fit into a larger pattern of Western amnesia about the conflict between Islam and Christianity, and of fashionable Western self-loathing. Muslims have offered no apologies. Some Muslim leaders still call the faithful to counter-crusade today,

---

8. Ibid., 211.

The Power of Forgiveness

viewing themselves as continuing the tradition of Muslim conquest of Christian lands (though many of those lands have ceased to be Christian in any meaningful way). Muslims in general seem to have accepted the Christians' self-description as unjust aggressors.[9]

I agree with Crawford that there is a current trend in the West to take the blame for all the problems in the world. I have often noticed this in the news. And there is no question that Muslims started the conflict against Christians. This can easily be proved by reading church history, starting a few centuries before the Crusades began. And Crawford's point that "Muslims have offered no apologies" is right on the money. Of course they have offered no apologies! Why would Islamic leaders apologize? They are merely being consistent with their history and their religion. Muhammad never went back to any of the villages that he burned to the ground to say, "I'm sorry"!

But therein lies the point. Forgiveness is an essential message of Christianity. It's what we do. Jesus forgave, and he commanded his followers to forgive. "I tell you who hear me: Love your enemies, do good to those who hate you, bless those who curse you, pray for those who mistreat you. . . . If you love those who love you, what credit is that to you? Even 'sinners' love those who love them" (Luke 6:27–28, 32).

Forgiveness, however, is not an essential message of Islam. The Muslims we have talked to about the Crusades are fully aware of the fact that Islam was as violent and out of control as

9. Paul Crawford, "A Deadly Give and Take," *Christian History & Biography*, April 1, 2002, 24.

Christianity was. Moreover, they see that in many cases today Islam is still violent and out of control.

So I am in favor of us, as believers, taking the high road and asking to be forgiven, whether or not Muslims ask us to forgive them. It doesn't matter. Our asking them to forgive us is not dependent upon them asking us to forgive them. That's what makes us different. Jesus told us that clearly.

You may be wondering what this has to do with you. Here is how God can use this in your life. If you have a friend who is a Muslim, bring up the subject of the Crusades sometime in a conversation. Just bring it out in the open, and let him or her know that you have read about the wars between Christians and Muslims in the Middle Ages. Then admit that this is exactly the opposite of what Jesus called us to do. You might share the words from Luke 6:27–28, 32 above. What is important is for your Muslim friend to hear Jesus' words. The sheer power of the Word of God will make an impact on his or her heart.

One day I was in Iran visiting on the streets with two young men in the Iranian army. After we talked awhile, I said, "I am a Christian; and you are probably from the Muslim religion, right?"

"Yes!" both young men eagerly replied.

I said, "Recently I have been reading some church history— about the Crusades in particular."

Though they were only in their early twenties, they knew all about the Crusades. By the way, this is often a popular topic in sermons in mosques throughout the Middle East, as we have been told by Muslims we have interviewed. We have heard such sermons ourselves, translated for us by Arabic friends, while praying around mosques during Friday prayers. As you can imagine, Islamic clerics, when preaching about the Crusades, omit the atrocities that Muslims committed before the Crusades, during the Crusades, and after the Crusades.

"I think this period of history was a terrible time for us as Christians, because we did not follow what Jesus told us to do," I continued. Then I referred to Peter's questioning Jesus about forgiveness (found in Matthew 18:21–22). "The Bible records the story of one of his disciples asking Jesus how many times his followers are to forgive others. 'Lord, how many times shall I forgive my brother when he sins against me? Up to seven times?' But Jesus answered by saying, 'I tell you, not seven times, but seventy-seven times.'

"Isn't that amazing? We were clearly wrong during the Crusades. We should have extended forgiveness rather than retaliation, don't you think? So will you please forgive us for the Crusades?"

At that point the young men were speechless. But after they gave it some thought, they said, "Yes, we forgive you."

I went on with the conversation. "You have probably seen people of your religion do things that that you were ashamed of also."

Immediately one of the young men replied, "We are ashamed at what happened when the subways were blown up in London and when America was attacked on 9/11. That was not right." His friend nodded in agreement.

We went on to have a great discussion for about an hour. The message of forgiveness really resonated with them. We even talked about the gravity of the continual news that America and Iran may go to war, in light of the fact that they are in the Iranian army. Not only do they hope a war is avoided, but both of them also have cousins in the United States who love living there. One day they would like to visit America.

I continue to communicate with these two young soldiers via e-mail. Their eyes have been opened, and they are asking more questions about Jesus.

This is why forgiveness is so powerful. Here we were talking openly about Jesus, Islam, and the threat of war between our two countries. I believe that the message of forgiveness made all of this happen. Asking for forgiveness is humbling, but it has the power to break down walls between us and the Islamic community worldwide. And that power comes across loud and clear in the Middle East, where bitterness from past hurts simply won't go away.

From Darfur to Jerusalem

Recently I was speaking with a Sudanese refugee living in Israel. "Sudan hates Israel!" Ahmed said. "Our leaders have the same view of Israel as the leaders of Iran. We just don't have any money to do anything about it. Our country has training camps for terrorists who hope to fight against Israel someday. Our Sudanese passports even say 'Valid for all countries except Israel.' That I would end up in Israel is a miracle. That I would end up in Israel *and be welcomed here* is a greater miracle."

Ahmed is like many of the other Sudanese who have escaped from the bloody strife in Darfur and made it all the way through Egypt and into Israel. There are about four thousand Sudanese refugees living safely in Israel. The Sudanese have had enough persecution and strife in their own country to last for centuries. They can't get a break even when they try to leave. In a March 5, 2008, article in the *Sudan Tribune*, Dr. Abdullah Osman El-Tom, who is from Sudan, wrote about the growing phenomenon of the Sudanese refugees who make the marathon trek to Israel.

If Darfur asylum seekers do not feel safe in Cairo, they cannot fare any better at the Israeli-Egyptian border. Their enemies are not "the evil Jews" as we have been taught at schools since early childhood. Rather, it is the lethal weapons of the Egyptian border guards that are responsible for the damage. Occasionally, border guns are saved and the killing is done by hand. Here is a testimony of an Israeli border guard describing actions of his Egyptian counterparts:

"The Egyptians passed the two refugees from one to another, beating them. We saw them gang up on them and beat them on the ground until they stopped moving. . . . They killed two men with their own hands and sticks and rocks. We heard them crying and screeching in pain until they died."[10]

---

10. Abdullah Osman El-Tom, "From Darfur to Israel," *Sudan Tribune*, March 5, 2008.

In all fairness, we have also heard stories about Egyptian soldiers refusing to shoot these defenseless people. One Sudanese refugee heard an Egyptian soldier call a major on his cell phone and say, "I will not shoot them. They are families."

Ahmed had quite a scare when he approached the border. He recounted his sprint for the Israeli border while being chased by Egyptian soldiers.

"Remember, my whole life I had been told that Israel was the enemy. But we had heard that they were helping our people from Sudan, and there was nowhere else to go. I could see the Philadelphia Corridor, which is the Israeli buffer zone between Egypt and the Gaza Strip. As I was running at full speed and fearing that my life was about to end, I could hear the Israeli soldiers on the other side of the fence cheering. They were cheering for me! I cannot forget the words they were yelling at the top of their lungs: 'Come on. You can make it!'"

On the other side of the fence was a young messianic believer named Sarah, who was in her second year in the Israeli army. She prayed for Ahmed as he raced toward the fence. *Lord, please spare his life. While he is here, bring believers to him who will share with him your love and message of salvation.*

Sarah's prayers were answered. Ahmed made it across the border, though he was soon placed in a refugee camp. Of course, he was glad to be safe and have food to eat. One day a Jewish believer visited him in the camp and gave him a Bible. Ahmed read the New Testament.

He recounts, "I read Jesus' words 'Love your enemies.' And then it hit me: this happened to me; my enemies loved me. At that point I realized that Jesus' message was true. I am living proof of Jesus' love and forgiveness. I was more than willing to put my trust in Jesus Christ for salvation. I thought I was merely running away from the Egyptians who wanted to kill me just because I am from Sudan. In reality, I was running to Jesus, who set me free from my sins through his forgiveness."

Farah—A Lesson in Forgiveness

Jesus told us to forgive our enemies. In the Middle East, everyone has an enemy. Can Jesus really give you the power to forgive someone who hates you? Can he give you the power to forgive someone who killed someone in your family? What about the power to forgive someone who killed your *whole* family?

Farah grew up in Iraq. She had a good life with her loving husband, Ali, and their three daughters. As a Muslim she never really considered the claims about Jesus, assuming they were only relevant for the small Christian minority in her country. The war with the United States began in 2003. Ali had served in the national army during the first Gulf War, but this time he was able to avoid doing so. Farah feared that he soon would be called up and required to put the Iraqi uniform on once again.

For a while everything went all right, and Farah even spent more time with her husband than she thought possible considering the country was at war. But when terrorist groups began to strike at will in Baghdad, her neighborhood became unsafe, and Farah wished she could flee to someplace safer for her children. Her relatives, who lived north of Baghdad, decided that because of the intensity of the war and because Farah and Ali lived so close to the Green Zone, they should pack up the children and stay with them for the time being.

Ali agreed, and he had heard at work that a major campaign to root out terrorists was about to begin. With more military closings and travel for Iraqis becoming restricted, in a few days it might be impossible to leave. It looked like now or never. In about two hours Ali and Farah pulled together the essentials, and Ali drove their car north toward the home of Farah's relatives. Because of his military experience, Ali knew the best way to get there. The road he chose had only one checkpoint. Once they were through it, they would be safe.

When they reached the checkpoint, the American soldiers, as usual, told them to get out of their car so they could inspect the vehicle for weapons or bombs. While they were standing by the side of the road with their hands over their heads, a car coming from the same direction sped toward the checkpoint. Shots began firing in both directions. It was a suicide mission.

The whole family hit the ground as the battle intensified ferociously. There was no place to hide, and the five of them clung to each other in the midst of the assault. Soon another vehicle sped toward the checkpoint. The last thing Farah remembered hearing was her youngest daughter calling out, "Mommy! Mommy!" Then there was silence.

Farah opened her eyes to a scene that would change her life. Her world of sadness began when she realized amid all the carnage that her husband and all three of her daughters were dead in the street. An American soldier had accidentally shot all four of them when the terrorists' car careened out of control right behind them. With a combination of overwhelming grief and anger, Farah screamed, "No!"

But it was too late. Her entire family was gone.

The next few months Farah lived with her relatives, not able to bear the thought of going back to her home. The pain was too fresh. Her tears had not subsided in the least. Her life was over. She hated America. She hated the American military. They had ruined her life.

While staying with her relatives, Farah met a neighbor who was a follower of Jesus. Ruba was also a widow, and she reached out to Farah. The two of them spent long hours talking. Farah was amazed that even though Ruba had suffered so much after losing her husband, there was something different in her outlook. Ruba had a hope that Farah did not possess. One day their conversation turned to Allah, and Ruba confessed to Farah that it was only because of Jesus that she could go on. Her Savior gave her the will to go on; he was the hope in her life. Eventually Ruba led Farah to give her life to Jesus.

Farah began attending a local fellowship, and the believers ministered to her daily. She began to devour the Bible, and her faith in Jesus became so real that he became her best friend. One of the women in the group planned to attend a women's conference in Jordan, and she invited Farah to go with her. The small church took up an offering and raised the money for the trip.

When Farah arrived, she was surprised to meet a team of believers from the United States who were helping to lead the conference. It was hard for her at first to be among the Americans. It was an American marine who had taken away her precious Ali and left her without her three sweet little girls. But she prayed and smiled as she met the women from the United States.

To break down the walls, the American team used the "ministry of touch" with their Arab sisters in Christ, massaging their hands, giving them facials, and painting their fingernails. As Diane's turn to give facials drew near, she was nervous. She had heard Farah's story about how an American marine had killed her whole family. Diane's son was a marine and had just finished serving in Baghdad. She prayed for the words to say if Farah ended up in her chair. Over eighty women were attending the conference, so the chances were slim, but she wondered what she would do if God called her to minister to Farah. What would she say?

After lunch Diane went to her chair, and she was speechless as she saw Farah heading straight for her. She couldn't get out of this one. She prayed and asked God for the words to say.

Farah shared her story, which lasted through the whole facial. When she was done, Diane blurted out, "I have a story too, Farah. My son just finished serving in Iraq with the American military. He is a marine." An awkward quiet came over the whole room.

Diane went on to say, "I am so sorry about what happened to your family. I cannot believe the pain you must be going through. I am so sorry."

Both of them were crying now, as Farah looked at Diane and said, "I am sure he must be a very nice young man."

The two of them wept together in each other's arms. Several minutes went by before they spoke again. In silence they continued to communicate from their hearts. The two sisters in Christ comforted each other.

Farah and Diane keep in contact with each other. Their bond in Christ is strong, and the love they have for each other continues to grow. Only their Father in heaven could have arranged their meeting. Only Jesus in Farah's heart could have filled her with love and forgiveness for the mother of an American soldier. Even though Diane's son had nothing to do with the death of her husband and daughters, bitterness could have captured Farah's heart. But it didn't—because Farah was now free.

Then you will know the truth, and the truth will set you free.

Jesus speaking in John 8:32

6

The Dangerous Privilege

"No servant is greater than his master." If they
persecuted me, they will persecute you also.

Jesus speaking in John 15:20

"The persecution of believers in the Middle East is the worst I have experienced in the past twenty years. If you are going to bring the gospel to Muslims here, you have to get rid of any fear. Only Christ can take away our natural tendency to be afraid when imprisonment, torture, and martyrdom are a real possibility."

The seasoned Christian leader who spoke these words lives somewhere in the Middle East, and he ought to know about persecution. His phone is constantly tapped; and he has been followed, interrogated, imprisoned, and beaten. When I met Jamal about eight years ago, one of the first things he said to me was, "You have to be a little crazy to serve Christ in the Middle

East!" Jamal said this with a big smile on his face, but he wasn't kidding.

Jamal's personality and attitude radiate the love of Christ. The joy on his face lights up a room. He is called to be on the frontlines for Christ, where he is passionately driven to take Jesus and his message throughout the entire Middle East. His life has been tough. "I think every Christian should go to jail at least once for his or her faith in Christ," he says. "After that, the only thing left for them to do to us is kill us. But that is the best blessing of all. Once they kill us, we are with Jesus forever!"

Many Christians throughout the world suffer under persecution or the threat of it. Britain's MI6 intelligence service released a report in June 2007 detailing the extent of Christian persecution worldwide. It estimated that 200 million Christians in sixty countries are now facing persecution.[1]

In Pakistan, Sajid William was murdered by Muslim fundamentalists in Peshawar in January 2008. He worked for Shelter Now, a Christian ministry in the region. After shooting him three times in the chest, the killer used William's cell phone to call the victim's wife to tell her of the murder. In 2005 Pastor Babar Samson, along with his driver, was murdered on the way to a church meeting.[2] Babar had discipled new believers for years and was one of the most influential leaders in Pakistan.

---

1. *Joseph Farah's G2 Bulletin*, June 2, 2007, WorldNetDaily.com; quoted in "News on the Persecuted Church," LetUsReason.org, http://www.letusreason. org/Persecut.htm.

2. "Young Christian Evangelist Murdered in Peshawar," International Christian Concern, January 23, 2008, http://www.persecution.org/suffering/ newsdetail.php?newscode=6914.

The Dangerous Privilege

A Muslim I befriended in Iran told me about incredible abuses of Christians in prison. He worked for the government and was horrified at what he saw when he visited a jail in the Tehran area. A moderate Muslim, his heart went out to the Christians who were beaten mercilessly. He showed me a gruesome photograph he had secretly taken of a prisoner who, as a lesson for the other prisoners, had been tortured and then killed by hanging in front of the prison cells.

In 2005 Muslim terrorist groups launched a campaign to rid Iraq of its Christian population. Simultaneous bombings took place at local churches during that year throughout the Baghdad area, and Christians were targeted for kidnapping. As a result, the US State Department reported that approximately 200,000 Christians left Iraq or fled to the north.[3]

It is difficult to tabulate the number of martyrs worldwide. But if the findings of Great Britain's intelligence service are accurate and 200 million Christians worldwide are facing persecution, then the estimate that 250,000 Christians are martyred for their faith every year doesn't sound unreasonable. That would mean that about 684 believers are martyred every day, or about 29 every hour.

Today Jesus' church is facing perhaps the worst persecution in two thousand years. During the first century, the church experienced most of its persecution from the government of the ruling Roman Empire. In the first three decades of the church's existence, it was actually given some protection. It was during

---

3. "Iraq Country Report," International Christian Concern, http://www.persecution.org/suffering/countryinfodetail.php?countrycode=22.

this time that the apostle Paul asked a Roman centurion, "Is it legal for you to flog a Roman citizen who hasn't even been found guilty?" (Acts 22:25). The answer, of course, was no. Roman citizenship was a great benefit for Paul the missionary to have while traveling around the empire. But that would soon change.

In his work known as the *Annals*, the Roman historian Tacitus, who lived between about AD 56 and 117, recorded how much the mood in Rome changed in just a few years: "First those who confessed to being Christians were arrested. In their deaths they were made a mockery. They were covered in the skins of wild animals, torn to death by dogs, crucified or set on fire—so that when darkness fell they were burned like torches in the night."[4]

This first persecution was at the hands of the emperor Nero, who was known for his brutality even toward his own family. He had his adoptive brother and even his mother executed. The Christians thought surely the killing spree would end when Nero died in AD 68. Yet it continued. In 80 the famous Roman Coliseum was completed, capable of seating about fifty thousand spectators. Although it was used for various events, it became known as the killing place of Christians. Persecutions were well attended and became somewhat of a sporting event for Rome. In some cases believers were thrown into the arena with hungry lions and bears while the crowds cheered at their deaths.[5] The

---

4. Tim Dowley, ed., *Eerdmans' Handbook to the History of Christianity* (Grand Rapids: Eerdmans, 1977), 71–73.
5. Ibid., 73.

courage of these men and women who followed Christ to the point of death inspires and motivates me.

The church experienced ten major persecutions at the hands of the Romans in the first three hundred years of its history. The Christian classic *Foxe's Book of Martyrs* contains a profound statement about the suffering of Jesus' church. "The history of Christian martyrdom is, in fact, the history of Christianity itself; for it is in the arena, at the stake, and in the dungeon that the religion of Christ has won its most glorious triumphs." Foxe goes on to say, with respect to the brave individuals who gave their lives, "We witness a soul so under the influence of good, that evil, even in its most cruel form, cannot dim its beauty, but serves as a constant to heighten its luster."[6]

Today persecution is not centered in an empire or in one city. Persecution is happening all over the globe. In February 2008 Voice of the Martyrs published its annual World Watch List. Here is this year's ranking of the ten worst places for Christians to live:

1. North Korea——Communist

2. Saudi Arabia——Muslim

3. Iran——Muslim

4. Maldives——Muslim

5. Bhutan——Buddhist

6. Yemen——Muslim

---

6. John Foxe, *Foxe's Book of Martyrs*, 15th printing (Old Tappan, NJ: Fleming H. Revell Company, 1979), 5.

7. Afghanistan——Muslim

8. Laos——Communist

9. Uzbekistan——Muslim

10. China——Communist[7]

Gaza in the Vise Grip

Even though the Gaza Strip was not listed in the top ten countries for persecuting Christians, the church in Gaza is in a terrible situation. Now that Hamas is ruling, there is no protection whatsoever for the believers. When the Palestinian Authority was in charge, there was limited protection; but that disappeared when Hamas was elected to power in January 2005.

This is what the Gaza Baptist Church experienced in just one year, the year 2007:

- The bus driver for the children's Awana club was killed.
- The church's guard was wounded and hospitalized.
- The church was taken over twice by the Palestinian Authority in its fight against Hamas.
- The Bible society, an extension of the church, was firebombed. Later it was blown up.
- Several times the church was riddled with bullets, and bullets flew through the windows during services and during Awana.

---

7. "North Korea: Number 1 Persecutor of Christians," Voice of the Martyrs Australia, February 18, 2008, http://www.persecution.com.au/news/article.asp?artID=%7B86EC558B-77B0-4274-9389-8F65D02B5B66%7D.

- Several leaders were threatened and told they were being "watched" by various terrorist groups.
- Rami Ayyad, who worked at the Bible society, was martyred on October 7, 2007.

The leaders of this church continue to receive threats almost daily from Islamic terrorists. And you thought your church had problems.

These believers are passionate about taking a stand for Jesus Christ no matter how difficult life gets. Just when the living situation in this small area (roughly twenty-six miles long by six miles wide) seems like it can't get any worse, it does. Just as I was writing this section, I received a Google alert about Gaza. Hamas fired ninety rockets into Israel during the last forty-eight hours, and the Israelis will certainly retaliate. The church is caught in the middle of the conflict.

Reading the list above and realizing all these Christians have been through in one year makes you wonder how anyone can live this way. Nobody can. If Jesus wasn't living in the believers, it would be more than impossible. But they are victorious and overcoming the resident evil in the Gaza Strip. Muslim terrorists have tried to put the church out of commission for decades, but Christians continue to live for Jesus and be his hands and feet in that difficult place.

Pastor Hanna Massad has led the Gaza Baptist Church for the last decade. He is a shepherd, a teacher, and a godly, determined leader. The church shares Christ with people whether they are nominal Christian or Muslim. Here are just a few of the ways that this amazing ministry center meet needs in Gaza:

- They have a library that is used by thirty thousand people.
- They feed some of the people in the refugee camps. A staggering number of refugees—about half a million— live in eight camps in Gaza.
- They have a school, kindergarten to twelfth grade, that is open to both Christians and Muslims.
- They have a health clinic. The women's clinic includes a mammogram machine and a nurse to assist the women. There is only one other machine in all of Gaza.
- They have 160 children in their Awana children's club.
- They have a Bible distribution center run by the Bible society.
- They are building a computer lab to teach job skills.
- They host leadership training classes for the Palestinian Authority.
- They share Jesus.

It would be easy to conclude from the news we hear from the Middle East that all the people in Gaza are either terrorists or have a terrorist in their family. The residents of the Strip talk openly about what it's like to have terrorist groups living among them—groups like Hamas, Fatah, Islamic Jihad, Hezbollah, and al-Qaeda, as well as other new, developing groups. But there are also goodhearted Muslim people living in Gaza who want nothing to do with eradicating Israel. Number one on their priority list simply would be to have a better life.

After the Bible society was blown up last year, believers in Gaza witnessed a miracle. Three hundred people gathered to protest the unfair targeting of the ministry that had done so much for the community. The leaders of this ministry did much more than hand out Bibles. They counseled families and individuals. They gave away food. They helped struggling families pay their utility bills. They prayed with residents. They helped in any way they could to meet the enormous needs in this area with an unemployment rate that is estimated at 35 percent.

The miracle was that the people in the crowd that assembled and marched down the main streets of Gaza City that day were Muslim. They realized the injustice of the situation, and they were not about to sit by with no reaction. The building where many of them had sought help was now in shambles.

"Muslims came to the defense of Christians in the Gaza Strip," one of the astonished church leaders told me. "We were surprised that the people who marched were not punished or, even worse, killed for making this statement."

Into the Heart of Terrorism

Afghanistan and Pakistan, two countries in the heart of central Asia, have a long history of Islamic fundamentalism. Pakistan is currently the only Islamic state that has nuclear weapons. The fact that these weapons are in the hands of an Islamized military is a severe threat to global security. The al-Qaeda terrorist network is also calling the people of Pakistan to follow the way of jihad.

This region is ripe for an Islamic revolution that threatens the entire world. Afghanistan has the Taliban, which once looked defeated but has rallied and is now growing again. Adding Iran, just to the west of Afghanistan, to the mix makes this region a hotbed of hard-line Islam.

The continual threat of terrorist groups makes serving Christ in central Asia extremely dangerous. But the good news is that the church is growing. Repeated Islamic-generated violence is having an adverse effect on moderate Muslims in both Afghanistan and Pakistan. Having lived through several decades of war and tribal battles, the typical Muslim family in central Asia is weary and longing for a better life. The region is ripe not only for an Islamic revolution but also for an advancement of the gospel.

In 2003 a taxi driver named Ahmad in central Asia (exact location withheld for security reasons) met an American. He was able to speak enough broken English to have a short conversation with John. Ahmad told John he was glad American soldiers were in the region. He said that he was glad they had defeated the Taliban and that he hoped they would defeat al-Qaeda next. The two began a friendship, and soon John shared his faith in Christ with Ahmad. John was surprised that Ahmad, being a Muslim, was ready to commit his life to Jesus the first time he witnessed to him.

Ahmad began devouring the Bible and meeting with John whenever he could. God equipped this young man to become an effective evangelist. One by one, Ahmad led disenchanted young Muslims to Christ. He started meeting with other believers and discipling them. Ahmad needed help as the numbers grew. That help would come from an unlikely source.

One day as Ahmad was driving through the city, he spotted an old friend. Ali needed a ride, so Ahmad picked him up. Ahmad noticed that Ali was more nosy than usual, as he started looking through the glove compartment. Ali found Ahmad's Bible, appearing shocked when he realized what it was.

"Ahmad, what are you doing with this?"

"It's mine, Ali. I read it every day." That was a bold statement considering that Ali had become involved in a terrorist group.

Ali responded, "I've always been interested in the Christian religion. And I suppose it wouldn't hurt to read the Bible, would it, Ahmad?"

Ahmad refused to let his friend borrow the Bible because it was the only copy that he knew of and because he was afraid Ali wouldn't give it back.

"Can't I just have it for a week?" Ali begged.

"Absolutely not!" Ahmad exclaimed.

Ali continued to bargain, and finally Ahmad gave in and agreed to let Ali have his Bible for one hour. Ali promised that Ahmad could run his errands and then come back and pick up his Bible. An hour later Ahmad was on Ali's doorstep, but no one answered the door even though he pounded and pounded on it.

This routine went on day after day for two weeks, and Ahmad was fit to be tied. He decided to stay at Ali's front door until he got his Bible back. He continued knocking until Ali's nephew finally opened the door. At five years old, he wasn't very good at covering up. He said, "My uncle told me to tell you that he is not home!"

Ahmad started laughing and walked through the doorway. He found Ali in his bedroom—on his knees and with tears in his eyes, Ahmad's Bible open in front of him.

"I haven't left my home in two weeks, Ahmad. I am sorry I kept your Bible, but I couldn't stop reading it. I love Jesus now."

Once again Ahmad was overwhelmed by the power of God: Ali was a new creation in Christ.

Today Ahmad and Ali are in one of the most difficult areas of central Asia. The two of them are pastoring over six thousand new believers, the majority of them under the age of twenty-five. They have started over forty churches, which have gone underground to protect the growing flock. Ahmad and Ali represent the new breed of spiritual leaders in central Asia.

Recently Ahmad and Ali have been targeted by the resurging Taliban. Miraculously, both of them have survived and are faithfully serving Christ in central Asia, even though the terrorist group has threatened to kill them.

The Power of a Disciple

Hanna Massad, pastor of the Gaza Baptist Church, shared these words relative to persecution with a group of us during a recent visit to Gaza: "The Bible uses the term *Christian* less than ten times. But it uses the term *disciple* over two hundred times. That's what we are called to be—disciples. So in the difficult places in the world we are well aware that there is great danger in serving Christ as his disciples. Jesus never ran away from danger, and neither will we."

His Name Is Osama —The Good Osama!

He is a one-man revolution. Maybe it goes with the name Osama. He is revolutionary in his approach to dealing with Muslims. He is on the edge, but effective. For security reasons, let's just say he lives somewhere in the Middle East.

Osama was a radical Muslim, and his life goal was to be a part of the big jihad. The Islamic clerics in his country told him that one day the Muslims would rule the world and that everyone would bow to Allah and his prophet Muhammad.

Osama decided to go for broke. His whole life was dedicated to following the religion of Islam. He memorized the entire Koran. He faithfully prayed five times a day. He made the hajj to Mecca. Osama was not an uneducated man. He decided to become a physician. His grades were excellent. His commitment to Islam was flawless. His heroes were the most radical Islamic leaders in the world. He liked very much that his name was Osama. His destiny was set in stone. Nothing could alter his course.

But God did. Osama began to have dreams and visions. He couldn't explain them to anyone. Who would understand? They would say he was making it all up. They could kill him and his family. But the dreams were real. The first dream was about Jesus, who was dressed in a white robe. He told Osama that he wanted to forgive his sins and make him clean on the inside. Shaken by the encounter, Osama couldn't get it out of his mind. *How could anyone say they had the power to forgive sins? Even Muhammad never said that. No one can know if their sins are forgiven.*

Osama wondered if this was really Jesus. *Why would the prophet Jesus want anything from me?* But the dreams continued. Osama felt drawn to Jesus. "The feeling that I had during each dream was one of complete peace," he says. "I was overjoyed, and I wanted to stay there with Jesus. I wanted to learn from him. I wanted to follow him."

The dreams picked up in their intensity and started to occur almost nightly. On one hand, Osama was on the path to becoming a hard-line Muslim leader. On the other hand, his heart was being softened by Jesus. He wasn't acquainted with any believers. There was no one to ask about the dreams.

One night Osama was out late with friends; and as he drove home, he kept seeing someone standing in the road in front of his car. He would slow down, and then the person was gone. This happened several times. Osama thought that he was losing his mind. He pulled the car over and parked. Maybe he wasn't feeling good.

From three o'clock until eight o'clock Osama stayed in his car. He couldn't move. For five hours he had an ongoing vision of Jesus. Jesus talked to him and told him how much he loved him. As Jesus revealed to Osama some of his sins, Osama wept. The vision was intense, and it was glorious. When it was over, Osama was exhausted. He sat in his car and gave his life to Jesus; he asked Jesus to forgive his many sins. On the way home he felt that he was floating in the air. He was crying tears of joy and singing at the top of his lungs about how he loved Jesus. He was forgiven, and his life was changed.

At that time Osama didn't know even one Christian. The day after his vision he met three believers! All of them had experienced dreams and visions also. One of them had a Bible. They decided to meet secretly—four followers of Jesus coming together to worship him in the dark of night.

The four committed themselves to share their faith daily, and they asked God to bring people to them who needed to hear of his love. Each day they saw God move in people's hearts, and their nightly meetings grew until the home in which they met was packed. It seemed that every young person they talked to was interested in learning more. They opened up about how dissatisfied they were with Islam. God was remote rather than personal; they longed for a relationship with a loving Father.

One night a man came to the meeting and told the group that he was sick of Islam and that he wanted to know more about Jesus. They told him about their experiences, and Osama detailed his vision to the man. The meeting lasted all night. The next day Osama was awakened by someone knocking on his door. At least thirty policemen were standing in front of his home. Osama was arrested for proselytizing Muslims and thrown in jail.

In prison he was beaten by fellow inmates every day and threatened by the guards. Osama was told his sentence would be for life. At age twenty-five, he prepared himself to live in jail for the rest of his days. Relatives pleaded for a reduced sentence. His father knew someone in the government. Even though he was humiliated that his son was accused of converting to Christianity and converting others, he begged a government official to give Osama another chance. Much to Osama's surprise, one day a prison guard came to his cell and told him he was free to go.

Getting thrown in jail gave the young evangelist time to think about his life. If Jesus ever got him out of prison, he made a commitment to reach Muslims for the rest of his life. The believers' meetings have grown to the point where they are held in several locations during the middle of the night. Osama and his leadership team have trained young leaders, and the movement is growing. It now numbers in the thousands.

To make sure newcomers aren't police spies, they have a test. They open the Koran, lay it on the floor, and ask the newcomer to step on it. Osama explains, "No one who is practicing Islam would ever dare desecrate the book that is holy to them. They would be petrified to do that! It is the test that reveals what's really in their heart. If they are following Jesus or ready to give their heart to him, they will do so at any cost. And that means turning their back on Islam."

The new believers will be meeting tonight. The revolution continues.

I consider everything a loss compared to the surpassing greatness of knowing Christ Jesus my Lord, for whose sake I have lost all things.

Philippians 3:8

7

Divine Intervention

*This salvation, which was first announced by
the Lord, was confirmed to us by those who
heard him. God also testified to it by signs,
wonders and various miracles, and gifts of the
Holy Spirit distributed according to his will.*

Hebrews 2:3–4

Have you ever noticed that God gets blamed for a lot of
things? If you look at the average insurance policy, the ultimate
escape clause usually reads "hurricane, flood, tornado, or any
other act of God." To some, I suppose, the only thing God does
is wipe people out when they get out of line. The rest of the time
he is not involved in our lives at all.

On the other hand, when something happens that clearly
points to divine intervention, would your first response be to

give credit to God or to explain it away? I have to confess that before I began traveling to the Middle East I might have tried to explain miracles away. I had witnessed a few in my life, but the people who talked about miracles all the time seemed a little crazy to me. But a book on the breakthrough in the Middle East wouldn't be complete if it failed to mention the miraculous. God is working in the region in a way that is reminiscent of the first-century church. The miracles of God combined with the passion of the believers and the persecution they receive sound like something straight out of the Book of Acts.

A Desperate Generation

Until seven years ago, I had no idea that God would lead me to the mission field. That wasn't on my radar screen at all. As a pastor, I admired missionaries; but I was glad that God hadn't called me to be one.

The first missionary I can remember meeting served in Africa. Her name was Jill, and she worked in a difficult place in North Africa—especially for a blond-haired, blue-eyed single girl. I was studying at Biola College at the time, and I was given the assignment to drive Jill to a church in the Los Angeles area for a Sunday night service. Jill had locked the keys to her rental car inside the car, and campus security wasn't able to break into the vehicle.

Other students who planned to serve Christ in missions wanted to come along, so we packed my Chevelle Super Sport and headed down the freeway. Along the way, Jill told us about her life and what it was like to live in a village in Africa and to trust Jesus with everything from safety to food and water for each day. Jill apologized that she needed me to drive her to the church. But I sure didn't mind, because she told some of the most fascinating stories I had ever heard in my life. The church service was also great.

As we headed back to Biola, Jill said, "We need to pray that God gets the keys out of the car without having to break the window to get in. My flight leaves the LA airport at 7:00 a.m., and it's almost midnight now." Jill taught us some African songs as we were driving, and I was fascinated by how this young woman served Jesus in such a dangerous area.

When we arrived back at Biola, something amazing happened. While I was getting out of my car, Jill immediately walked up to her rental car and began praying. "Lord, please open this door," was her simple prayer.

I walked up to the car, a Toyota Corolla, and said, "Well, maybe my key will work." I stuck my car key in the lock, and to my astonishment the door opened!

Jill said, "Thank you, Father!" Then she grabbed the keys from inside the car, shut the door, and locked it. "Tom, there is no way that a Chevrolet key should fit a Toyota. Let's put your key in and try it again."

At this point I was still holding the key, staring at it in amazement. I stuck it in the door, and this time it didn't work! "What?! It just worked. How did that happen?"

The other four students and I stood there in shock. But Jill calmly said, "You know, in Africa, where I live, we don't have mechanics when we have car problems. We just have God!"

She hugged each of us, said goodbye, and then headed to the dorm to get a few hours of sleep. As she walked away, she looked back at the stunned group of college students and said something I will never forget: "Remember, Jesus has more than enough power for any situation in your life. Go to him with everything. He won't let you down."

The next day the story about the "miracle key" and how God had opened the door with the key that didn't fit circulated all over the campus. I learned that Jill had one thing in her life that I did not: *desperation*. She was desperate for God to work in her life—and he often did. Jill was like so many believers I have met in the Middle East: they are desperate for God. If God doesn't answer their prayers, they have nowhere else to turn.

As time passed, I assumed, unfortunately, that miracles like the one I experienced with Jill's rental car were just once-in-a-while things. In other words, "Don't count on God to do that all the time." As a result of this kind of thinking, I became less desperate in my prayers. And of course I failed to see the miraculous in my life very often. That is, until I went to the Middle East.

Is Anything Too Hard for God?

Kareem was born into a Catholic Palestinian family in Bethlehem. Somewhere along the way he became disillusioned with his faith. He lived near the Church of the Nativity, the traditional site of Jesus' birth, and grew tired of the endless lines of pilgrims kissing the star that marks the spot where Jesus is said to have been born. "This is all a joke!" he concluded. To his parents' dismay, Kareem became an atheist—an angry atheist at that. He thought Christianity was the most absurd thing on earth.

In his twenties and making good money, Kareem teased his friends for believing in what he thought was a fairy tale. He told them that going to church was just a waste of time. But then one of Kareem's friends asked him to go with him to an evangelical church and hear the new pastor. Surprisingly Kareem went, though only to laugh at the "poor, helpless people who are so deceived."

The people warmly welcomed Kareem, and he was surprised to see that civic leaders from Bethlehem—doctors, lawyers, and businesspeople—were also present. He had previously thought that Christians were uneducated folks who were gullible and manipulated by the pastor. Kareem stopped scoffing at the people; and during the sermon, God began to touch his heart. The pastor ended the service by asking those who wanted to trust Jesus as their Savior to come forward. Kareem thought to himself, *No one could ever get me to give my life to Jesus. He never existed anyway. How foolish these people are.* Kareem was about to learn that he was wrong.

"The pastor stood at the front of the church. I looked down the aisle and saw a man in a white robe standing next to him. He was looking straight at me. I asked my friend, sitting next to me, who that man was standing next to the pastor.

"'I don't see anyone standing next to the pastor,' my friend replied. 'He's alone up there.'

"But he wasn't alone. The man next to him was wearing a white robe, and his eyes appeared to be looking right through me. He said, 'I love you, Kareem. Come to me.'

"All I know is that when he spoke to me and his eyes met mine something overwhelmed my heart so strongly that I got out of my chair and ran down the aisle, sobbing like a baby. I couldn't resist him."

Kareem repented of his sins, including the pride and anger that had ruled his life. He has been serving Christ ever since.

He now lives in Hebron, one of the most dangerous areas of the West Bank. Kareem met fierce resistance when he began sharing the love of Jesus there. He has been beaten, but that hasn't stopped him from telling Muslims about Jesus. The going was tough, as he didn't find anyone who was truly interested for four years. The people he talked to told him to leave them alone, or they even threatened him.

Kareem finally did lead one Muslim to Christ. But as he was visiting with the man in the privacy of the man's home, Kareem heard an explosion down the street. His car had been blown up. Kareem walked the streets of Hebron that night until he found a taxi driver. The man was asleep in the car, but Kareem woke him and convinced him to drive the twelve miles to Bethlehem, where Kareem still lived at the time. He prayed until the morning hours. With this kind of persecution, he wondered how he could ever see more than a handful of believers in Hebron. He had been able to lead only one person to Christ, and now his car had been blown to smithereens in the midst of the city he hoped to reach for Jesus. Desperation set in.

After hours of prayer Kareem had an experience that would define the rest of his life. "In the midst of my praying, a peacefulness filled the room; and suddenly I was flooded with hope and joy. In a moment the despair was gone. I opened my eyes and heard a voice say, 'Soon there will be twelve churches in Hebron that are filled with believers who love me.'

"The voice I heard was the same one I heard in Bethlehem the day I gave my life to Christ. I went to the church in Bethlehem that day to make fun of Christians. But today I serve Christ, and he has promised that we will see churches like the one in Bethlehem come to life all over the West Bank."

Kareem is seeing those words become a reality, as churches have begun in Hebron. They are small, but God is gathering families together to worship him in this important biblical city. Jews regard Hebron as the holiest city, other than Jerusalem, in Israel. Muslims likewise view this as a city of major importance. Abraham, as well as his wife, Sarah, is buried in Hebron at the famous cave of Machpelah (see Genesis 23; 25:7–11). Since Abraham is the father of both Isaac and Ishmael, this burial complex has become one of the most disputed and dangerous places in Israel. Hebron has been an outpost of Islamic fundamentalism in the West Bank. Members of a small Jewish community risk their lives to reside in Hebron.

"Jews and Palestinians have to live together in Israel," Kareem observes. "There is no other way for us to exist. Neither the Arabs nor the Jews are leaving, so our problems are here to stay. Jesus is the only one who can bring a peaceful coexistence to the land of Israel. He took away my hatred for Jews and filled me with love for them. Likewise I hated Muslims, even though I lived among them in Bethlehem. Now my heart is wide open to the people of Islam also. When I see the word *Islam*, I remember this acronym: 'I Shall Love All Muslims.'

"Isn't it amazing that God would bring me to serve him in this major battleground between the two religions? This city needs Jesus' message of love and forgiveness. Hebron can be the place where people see that only Jesus can solve the four-thousand-year-old conflict between Jews and Arabs. Both of us are the descendants of Abraham. Jesus wants to tear down the walls between us and create 'one new man,' as Ephesians 2 tells us. Hebron will see this one day."

"Jesus Doesn't Come to Syria!"

Damascus, the capital of Syria, is one of the oldest continuously inhabited cities in the world. Life in Damascus is historically intertwined with Islam. Damascus is one of the most respected cities in the Muslim religion. Friday prayers have been a constant in the famed Umayyad Mosque since approximately AD 715. Also called the Grand Mosque, this Islamic house of prayer is rooted in history that spans over three thousand years.[1]

During the Old Testament period Damascus was the capital of the Aramean kingdom. Around 1000 BC Israel's King David

---

1. Hamdan Makarem, *The Tourist Guide of Syria* (Damascus: Syrian Arab News Agency Press, 2004), 20–28.

defeated the Arameans, striking down 22,000 of their soldiers. Damascus became subject to David during this time when the Lord gave him several victories beyond the borders of Israel (2 Samuel 8:3–6). David defeated King Hadadezer, whose name means "Hadad is my help." Hadad was the chief god of the Arameans, and his temple was located on the site where the Umayyad Mosque rests today.

Damascus seems to pop up in history throughout the ages. During the Roman era the site of the future mosque became the temple of Jupiter, who was called the greatest of the Roman gods. Next, during the Byzantine Christian era, the site became the location of a church honoring John the Baptist. The church housed a shrine that was said to contain the head of the prophet who baptized Jesus. Not far from the mosque is Straight Street, where the apostle Paul was converted to Christ; and a church commemorates the place where Paul was lowered from the city wall in a basket, shortly after his conversion, in order to escape from the Jews who wanted to kill him (see Acts 9:1–25). In 636 Islam conquered Damascus. For about seventy-five years Christians were allowed to worship at the church, until it was demolished and the Grand Mosque, the centerpiece of the Umayyad dynasty, was built in its place.[2]

I believe that the Umayyad Mosque stands as a symbol of the Islamic faith. Since it was built on the site of previous houses of worship throughout history, it speaks to Muslims of Islam's superiority over all other religions today.

---

2. Ibid.

Next to Muhammad, Saladin is perhaps the greatest Islamic conqueror. He led his army in many victories over the crusaders, recapturing Jerusalem in 1187 and bringing virtually all of the Holy Land back under Islamic control in 1192. Saladin died in Damascus and is buried right outside of the Umayyad Mosque. Now that's some symbolism: anyone who goes to the Grand Mosque today is acutely aware that Islam has conquered before and that it will conquer again.

So why would a Muslim who lives in Damascus and attends one of the most strategic and famous mosques in the world leave Islam and become a Christian? Well, he probably wouldn't. Not unless God did something dramatic and completely unexpected in his life. Enter Amir Hadad.

Amir was perfectly content to live out his Muslim faith in Damascus. He wasn't looking for anything else—until he met some Christians who lived in his neighborhood. He knew about many of their beliefs, and he knew that they were people who prayed continually. Amir encountered some family problems, and one day his neighbor Magdy asked him why his heart seemed so heavy. When Amir opened up to him, Magdy vowed to pray and fast for Amir. "He told me he was trusting God for a breakthrough with my problem," Amir recalls.

Within a week the family problems were significantly better. After that Amir and Magdy began to have a much closer friendship. "I want to have the passion for prayer that you have, Magdy," Amir said. "How did you get it?"

With an opening like that, Magdy couldn't resist. He briefly shared with Amir the story of how he became a follower of Jesus.

Amir continued to give Magdy prayer requests and ask more questions.

In the fall of 2007, one night Amir awoke with excruciating pain. He was rushed to the hospital, where medical tests revealed that he had acute kidney failure and was soon going to need a transplant. The situation looked hopeless, as Amir's family couldn't afford such a procedure. Amir told his family to call Magdy for prayer.

This illustrates one of the principles we've learned in our ministry in the Middle East: No one turns down prayer. It doesn't matter if the person is a Muslim, a Jew, or a Christian. Everyone needs prayer, and it is the ultimate way to communicate that you care.

Magdy felt a little nervous at first when he began to pray for Amir to be healed of the disease that was threatening his life. But then great boldness came over him as he pleaded with Jesus to heal Amir's body. Amir's immediate family was all there, and they bowed in respect. "I want you to come and pray with me often," Amir told Magdy.

To Magdy's surprise, Amir immediately got worse. The doctors said that the kidney problems were worse than they previously thought and that Amir's days were numbered. Magdy gathered his church, and they decided to call a corporate time of prayer and fasting for Amir. Then when they learned that he was in intensive care, the believers came together in an emergency meeting and pleaded with God for Amir's life.

Amir recounts the miracle that happened next. "I knew that I was going to die. I had heard my family talking about my funeral once when they thought I couldn't hear them. One night I nodded off to sleep, and then in the middle of the night I was awakened by someone talking. A man in a white robe was at the foot of my bed, and he said that he was Jesus. He had nail prints in his hands and in his feet. He said that he had heard the prayers of his followers. He told me that he was going to heal me for his glory, and he touched me. Then he was gone."

The next morning the doctors and the nursing staff were shocked, since Amir was coherent and seemed to be just fine. "Jesus did it!" Amir proclaimed. "He came to me last night and healed me!"

"I am sure the doctors thought I had lost my mind at that point. But they began to run tests on my kidneys, and they couldn't find anything wrong with them! They responded, 'It couldn't have been Jesus. If someone healed you, it must have been a good Muslim man. It wasn't Jesus.'"

"How do you know it wasn't Jesus?" Amir asked.

"Jesus doesn't come to Syria! This is a Muslim country, not a Christian country."

"I can prove to you that it was Jesus. Have you ever met a Muslim who had nail prints in his hands and in his feet?"

"At this point they were speechless. They never asked me about the matter again. Jesus gave me back my life, and I owe him everything. My family loves him now too."

Amir is a transformed man—and rightfully so. He was at death's door, and Jesus brought him back to serve him.

Today Amir and his family host a church that meets in their home. God has used Amir's incredible testimony and his passion for Christ to reach other Muslims with the message of the gospel. Though it is dangerous to spread this message in Syria, Amir will not remain silent.

"Jesus spared my life when it was nearly gone. He has the power to change our hearts and make us into a new creation. I am proof of that, and so is my family. Thank you, Jesus, for coming to visit us in Syria! We will never be the same."

Jesus Loves the Little Children

We have also seen the miraculous power of God at work among children in the Middle East.

I love that our Savior had such affection for little ones. In Luke 18:15 we witness a wave of people rushing to bring their babies to Jesus to have him touch them. I'm sure they had seen Jesus perform miracles, and they thought if he could just touch them they would receive a blessing or maybe even a miracle. The disciples tried to keep these little ones away from Jesus. But he said, "Let the little children come to me, and do not hinder them, for the kingdom of God belongs to such as these. I tell you the truth, anyone who will not receive the kingdom of God like a little child will never enter it" (Luke 18:16–17).

Jesus was calling his followers to the innocence and faith inherent in children. And Jesus continues to have the same love for little children. Why would that change? I was reminded of this recently when a miracle happened to a three-year-old child in the Middle East.

Jasmine lives in Jordan. Her husband, Jamal, was a Muslim imam; but he became a believer after he began to have concerns about Islam. His questions were never answered. In fact, he was thrown in jail and beaten for asking them. "I was hung upside down and whipped with a rod every day that I was in prison. I just wanted to know the truth."

Jamal found Jesus through all of this and eventually became a Christian leader in the region. Jasmine has developed a women's ministry. She has become effective at leading women to Christ and then discipling them. She travels throughout her country, meeting with women who have many needs. Jasmine has often told us of the harsh treatment that many of these women have received, much of it coming from their husbands.

Jasmine has a heart full of love for the women of the Middle East; and since she shares her faith in Christ openly, there have been threats and attacks against her. She took medicine to women in one village who were in need of the medicine but unable to afford it. Jasmine escaped from being stoned in the village, which was 100 percent Muslim, yet went back a few days later. Her vehicle again was pelted with rocks, but she would not give up.

Jasmine told me, "God broke through their anger, and finally they stopped picking up rocks when I came. Now they welcome me with open arms. They are good people who just had misconceptions about Jesus and his followers. We have started a women's group in that village now."

When someone is sent to bring Christ to a certain people, God gives that person the ability to see life through the eyes of those people. Jasmine knew the villagers would come around one day and realize she was not a threat, but rather that she had been sent by God to help them. A church meets in the village now, and the people have seen the passion that the believers have to help them in practical ways. They have also come to believe that Jesus is watching over them and that he loves them very much. That message came through loud and clear at the time of a terrible accident.

After spending the day in the village, Jasmine hugged the women and prayed with them just before leaving. During the prayer time one of the women lost track of her three-year-old son, and he crawled under Jasmine's van to get a toy she had brought him. As she hopped in the van Jasmine asked, "Are all the children with their mothers?" Being assured that was the case, Jasmine started the engine and put the van in reverse. After traveling a few feet, she heard the screams that she will never forget the rest of her life.

The boy's mother had seen her son run into the house but didn't notice that he had come back outside. Jasmine had run over little Abdul, who now lay motionless on the ground. Thinking he was dead, the women fell on the ground and began weeping loudly. Jasmine was weeping too, but she pulled herself together as they loaded the boy into the back of the van, and she raced for the nearest hospital.

"Since we were so far from a city, there was no hospital within thirty miles. I raced down the highway, praying out loud the entire way to the hospital. There were six women in the van with me, and I could see them watching me through their tears as I poured out my heart to God."

Abdul was still unconscious when they arrived at the hospital, and he was rushed into the emergency room. Jasmine called her husband, Jamal, to send out a prayer alert. Within minutes believers all over Jordan were praying for little Abdul. Within an hour prayer groups around the Middle East were praying, and believers in the West were mobilized for intercession also.

Jasmine collapsed into Jamal's arms when he arrived at the hospital. She was overcome with grief that she might have caused the little boy's death. Jasmine had come to serve this desperate village, so it seemed cruel to her that this could happen. Jasmine and Jamal prayed throughout the night.

The doctors planned to operate on Abdul in the morning, saying that was his only hope for survival. But in the meantime Abdul woke up and told his mother that he was hungry. She almost fell out of the chair! The doctors came into his room; and after a quick check of his vitals, they wheeled him to x-ray. Then they said there must have been a mistake: the wheels of the van couldn't have rolled over Abdul, since there was no sign of internal injury.

Abdul's mother reminded the doctors, "You said that that the injuries were so great that he needed surgery this morning or he wouldn't survive. You saw his injuries yourselves. God did a miracle here! God answered the prayers of the Christians!"

Today Abdul shows no signs whatsoever of the accident. Because of Jasmine, the love of Jesus was already known in that Jordanian village. Now the power of Jesus is known there also. And many Muslims in the village now love Jesus.

Abraham Sarker—
Muslim Missionary to America

Abraham Sarker was born into a devout Sunni Muslim family in Bangladesh. His father was a leader in a prominent Islamic political party. His mother was a teacher in an Islamic school. Together they dreamed of raising their son to be a future Muslim leader. His parents spared nothing when it came to Abraham's religious education. Each young student of Islam is assigned a trainer to disciple them. Abraham's father wanted his son to have the best training, so he hired the imam of the local mosque to be Abraham's private tutor.

As a committed Muslim, Abraham memorized the Koran. He was curious about certain teachings in the Koran that puzzled him. But since Muslims are not allowed to question anything in the Koran, he kept his doubts to himself. When he was thirteen, he joined an Islamic organization and received additional training. As part of his training he gave the call to prayer at the local mosque. He climbed the minaret five times a day and called out the melodious Arabic chant: "Allah is great, Allah is great, come for prayer." Abraham was prepared to die for his faith, and he would have done so if called on in the name of Allah.

Like all Muslims, Abraham lived under the works system. His motivation to serve Allah was out of extreme fear. Later on, as a teacher, he passionately taught others that their only hope of attaining heaven was by doing enough good works to outweigh their sins. Deep inside, he knew no Muslim could ever really know whether he was going to an eternity in paradise or to an eternity in hell.

One night, during his teen years, Abraham had a dream that shook him to the core. He dreamed he died and was thrown into a lake of fire. All around him was blazing fire. He could feel his body burning, and the pain was indescribable. He was so shaken that he made a beeline for his parents' room and woke them. They assured Abraham that Satan was trying to disturb him and that he didn't have anything to worry about since he was such a good Muslim.

But he had the same dream again just a few nights later. Again feeling the fire burning his flesh, he screamed in anguish. Abraham needed some answers. *Why is this happening to me?*

This time he went to the imam who was mentoring him. The imam gave the same answer as his parents: Abraham was a good Muslim and had nothing to worry about. Because he was serving Allah, this was surely from Satan. And besides, he had done so many good things. Abraham hoped that the imam's words would soothe his fears. But they didn't. He was haunted by the dreams.

Abraham was now on a mission. If he was serving Allah with his whole heart, why did he have such doubt and insecurity? One Friday afternoon he remained at the mosque after Friday prayers. He demanded that God give him an answer. *I will not lift my head until you tell me the meaning of the dream.*

Abraham wanted to hear an audible voice, an answer from heaven to put his fears to rest. He waited and waited. Finally, while still in prayer at 4:30 in the morning, something strange began to happen. At first he heard a rushing wind all around him. Next, drops of rain began to fall on him. He looked around, and it wasn't "raining" anywhere else in the mosque! He began walking around, and the rain followed him wherever he went. His clothes became soaked. Soon his entire body was drenched. Abraham figured that there was a hole in the ceiling and that it was raining outside, but neither one was the case. The rain was falling on him and him alone!

This was no ordinary rain. It was an oil with a sweet fragrance that he had never smelled in his life. Abraham felt peace flooding over him. God had not answered his questions about the dream, but he felt that God had been there with him. Abraham was still in the mosque when the imam came in for the morning call to prayer. Immediately noticing the sweet fragrance, he said to Abraham, "Allah likes you."

Abraham was different from then on, and the nightmares of being thrown into hell never returned. One night he heard a voice say, "Get a Bible, Abraham." He looked around to see who had spoken, but he was alone on a deserted gravel road.

A Bible? How could he find a Bible? Muslims were not permitted to even read the Bible, and he didn't know where to find one. For four years he searched to find a Bible in the Islamic country of Bangladesh, but he never found one.

Then his father told him he wanted the whole world to believe in Islam; and because of this, he was going to send Abraham to America as a missionary. He would convert the infidels. His mother wished her son was going to Saudi Arabia so he could be surrounded by Muslims and not the godless Americans. She warned him that Americans ate pork, which is against Islamic dietary laws, and drank alcohol. Abraham would need to be careful. His mother even told him they put pork in cookies! With great sadness, he hugged his parents and family and boarded the plane for the United States.

Abraham found three roommates who were also Muslim missionaries, and they began their work on a college campus in Oklahoma. Even though Abraham was immersed in his missions work, he couldn't get the voice out of his head that had told him to get a Bible. He soon located the Baptist Student Union. And on the first shelf he looked at, to his amazement he found a Bengali Bible. This was unbelievable; Abraham didn't even know that a Bible in his own language existed! The translation was done by William Carey, "the father of modern missions." The leader of the campus ministry was shocked to find Abraham reading a Bible, since he was obviously a Muslim. "Why don't you take it? You can have it."

Abraham took the Bible, but he had to read it in the middle of the night in order to keep peace with his roommates. He immediately realized how different the Bible was from the Koran. For instance, it was Isaac who was to be sacrificed by Abraham—not Ishmael, like the Koran claimed. There were so many differences. He found Jesus to be loving and compassionate, unlike Muhammad, who was harsh and vindictive. After reading the Bible for a few nights, Abraham knelt by his bed and asked God to show him if he should follow Jesus instead of Muhammad. The next day he received his answer.

Another missionary was working on that campus. But Peter was a missionary *to* Muslims. He had lived in an Islamic country and was well versed in the Koran. At just the right time, as the

Holy Spirit was moving powerfully in Abraham's heart, God brought Peter and Abraham together. Peter answered Abraham's questions for hours. Finally, the sun began to dip beyond the horizon, and beautiful colors streamed across the sky.

Abraham thought about his family and how much he loved them. He knew this would hurt them terribly, but he could not deny the truth. Jesus was who he had been searching for his whole life. On the evening of April 14, 1992, Peter and Abraham knelt beneath a shade tree, and the young missionary from Bangladesh gave his life to Jesus Christ.

Salvation was free for Abraham, but it would cost him everything to follow his Savior. Because of his decision to follow Jesus, Abraham was thrown out of his apartment, rejected and disowned by his family, and beaten to the point of death by other Muslim missionaries while still living in Oklahoma. He not only survived all of this, but also flourished in his faith. Abraham has become a powerful evangelist, a Christian missionary to Muslims. He has a thriving ministry and has written a great book called *Understand My Muslim People*. Abraham's ministry website, GospelForMuslims.com, catalogs testimonies of Muslims who have found Jesus and are now living for their Savior. Abraham has continued his education and is a scholar in the field of apologetics.

Amazingly, Abraham Sarker *is* a missionary in America—just like his father wanted. The difference is that he now serves Jesus, the true and living God. God has done so much in his life. But outside of his salvation experience, the greatest miracle in Abraham's life happened just a few years ago. After years of being ostracized by his family and threatened by his father, Abraham and his wife, Amie, had the privilege of leading his dad to Christ. All the years of being isolated from his family and praying for them were worth it. Abraham's father is growing in his faith back in Bangladesh.

As I was writing this today, I received a call from Abraham. He had just returned from seeing his family and had great news. God blessed him even more, as he led his mother to faith in Christ after years of prayer and several spirited talks! How great the plans of the Lord were all along for the Sarker family. Our gracious Father sent Abraham halfway across the world in order to bring the love of Christ back home to his family.

> *You did not receive a spirit that makes you a slave again to fear, but you received the Spirit of sonship. And by him we cry, "Abba, Father." The Spirit himself testifies with our spirit that we are God's children. Now if we are children, then we are heirs—heirs of God and co-heirs with Christ, if indeed we share in his sufferings in order that we may also share in his glory.*
>
> Romans 8:15–17

Diagram of a Mosque

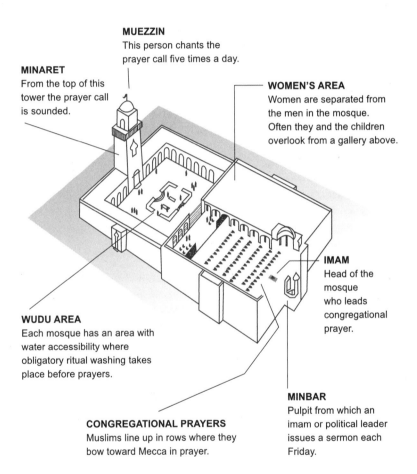

MUEZZIN
This person chants the prayer call five times a day.

MINARET
From the top of this tower the prayer call is sounded.

WOMEN'S AREA
Women are separated from the men in the mosque. Often they and the children overlook from a gallery above.

IMAM
Head of the mosque who leads congregational prayer.

WUDU AREA
Each mosque has an area with water accessibility where obligatory ritual washing takes place before prayers.

MINBAR
Pulpit from which an imam or political leader issues a sermon each Friday.

CONGREGATIONAL PRAYERS
Muslims line up in rows where they bow toward Mecca in prayer.

Used by permission.

8

Israel Does a 180

See, I lay in Zion a stone that causes men to
stumble and a rock that makes them fall, and
the one who trusts in him will never be put to
shame.

Romans 9:33

Israel is used to being attacked. The Israelis have fought six wars in the sixty years since becoming a nation in 1948. Their capital city of Jerusalem is at the center of peace negotiations once again, as many are pushing for it to be divided—Jewish on the western half and Arab on the eastern half.

Jerusalem means "city of peace." Yet it has had relatively little peace over the centuries. I believe the Messiah will reign there one day, and then peace will finally arrive for good. Until then it will remain the ultimate "city *without* peace." Throughout its history, Jerusalem has suffered at least fifty major sieges, sacks, captures, and destructions.[1]

We can read in the Old Testament that King Jehoshaphat had a big problem. Three nations came together with one common objective: to attack the king and his army in Jerusalem. The nation had divided in two, the southern kingdom of Judah with its capital of Jerusalem and the northern kingdom of Israel with its capital of Samaria. The Israelite lookouts who were positioned within ten miles of Jerusalem, in En Gedi, brought the dreaded news to the king: "A vast army is coming against you" (2 Chronicles 20:2).

Jehoshaphat's response is one of the finest examples of true spiritual leadership in the Old Testament. The king sought the Lord and asked for his direction in the matter, and he also called the nation of Judah to fast. The people responded and followed the king's lead. Jehoshaphat went into the courtyard of the temple and cried out to the Lord. His prayer ended with these words: "We have no power to face this vast army that is attacking us. We do not know what to do, but our eyes are upon you" (2 Chronicles 20:12).

How refreshing! What leader stands up and says, "I don't have a clue what to do here, but I am calling on God to help us out of this mess!" Jehoshaphat was godly enough to lay out the truth, no matter what the people thought. He humbled himself. With time running out, just a few hours before the threatening nations would attack, the prophet Jahaziel was given a message

---

1. Amos Elon, *Jerusalem: Battlegrounds of Memory* (New York: Kodansha America, 1995), 149.

from the Lord for the king and the people as they were gathered at the temple.

> Then the Spirit of the LORD came upon Jahaziel son of Zechariah, the son of Benaiah, the son of Jeiel, the son of Mattaniah, a Levite and descendant of Asaph, as he stood in the assembly. He said: "Listen, King Jehoshaphat and all who live in Judah and Jerusalem! This is what the LORD says to you: 'Do not be afraid or discouraged because of this vast army. For the battle is not yours, but God's.'" (2 Chronicles 20:14–15)

I think it's interesting that God's Word lays out the prophet's pedigree here. The Israelites had no time for some nutcase to stand up in the assembly and lead them astray. This was a true message from God via one of his prophets.

The king bowed to the ground and worshiped the Lord, and the people joined him. The next day the Lord defeated the three armies that came against Judah—and Jehoshaphat's troops didn't have to shoot a single arrow. When they arrived, their enemies were all dead. Afterward the nation came together at the temple for a national praise service complete with harps, lutes, and trumpets. Even though the nation had many periods of unfaithfulness and times of idolatry, when the people sought the Lord with their whole heart, the God of Israel came to their rescue.

Today Israel is once again surrounded by hostile peoples. To the north is Syria, under an Islamic military regime, and Lebanon, with its Hezbollah-led government. From the southwest Hamas launches missiles at Israel from the Gaza Strip almost daily. To the east Iran: and its president, Mahmoud Ahmadinejad, has promised to wipe Israel off the map. If you're a Jew who is living in Israel, could it get any worse?

Actually, it could. If you're a Jew who is living in Israel and you want to follow Jesus (or *Yeshua*, as his name is pronounced in Hebrew), your situation is even more dangerous. Best-selling author Joel Rosenberg asserts that the word *conversion* (i.e., to Christianity) brings about as much disdain among Jews in Israel as the word *pedophile* does in America.[2] He should know. He's a Jewish believer himself.

I've talked to many Jews in Israel who say they could never accept Jesus as their Messiah because if they did they would no longer be Jewish. I often respond by saying, "I accepted Jesus and I'm still Irish!" The answer is usually, "But we're Jewish, and that's different." They also say that they would be disowned by their parents because converting to Christianity is such a slap in the face to a Jewish family.

Jews still hold deep feelings of resentment toward the church. Many in the church, unfortunately, including some early church fathers, have made anti-Semitic remarks and even condemned the Jewish race. Justin Martyr said, "Kill the Jews!"[3] As I mentioned earlier, in the context of the historical relation-

2. Joel Rosenberg and Tom Doyle, "A Look at Modern-Day Israel," Focus on the Family radio broadcast, May 16, 2008.
3. David Dolan, *Israel at the Crossroads: Fifty Years and Counting* (Grand Rapids: Revell, 1998), 35.

ship between Jews and Arabs, John Chrysostom was even more insulting when he said, "Kill the pigs!" Origen claimed, "The synagogue is a brothel!"[4] On top of that, Martin Luther, the great Protestant reformer, was the first to call the Jewish race "filthy vermin."[5]

When you throw in the Crusades, the Spanish Inquisition, the Holocaust, and the fact that many leaders who have endorsed the killing of Jews claimed to be Christians, it's easy to see why Jews are horrified when someone in their family becomes a believer. But that barrier is coming down for Jews living in Israel today.

"Can Jesus Get Me a Job?"

Jonathan was a secular Israeli who wanted nothing to do with his Orthodox family background. Judaism just wasn't for him; and like so many other Israeli youth, he drifted away from anything traditional. Soon after Jonathan left home, he became involved in drugs and moved from one friend's home to another. Making a living was tough, but he was finally able to land a job in a business in Tel Aviv.

Jonathan had pulled it together; and even though he was a nonobservant Jew, he was sure that his family would be proud of him for at least nailing down a steady job with a decent income. But living in Israel's "anything goes" city catapulted Jonathan

4. John Hagee, *Final Dawn over Jerusalem* (Nashville: Thomas Nelson, 1998), 47.
5. Dolan, *Israel at the Crossroads*, 41.

into alcoholism, illicit sex, and more drugs. The saying in Israel is "You go to Jerusalem to pray, but you go to Tel Aviv to play."

Jonathan played hard, but the results of his hard partying left him empty and lonely. He got fired from his job and was running out of money. He considered moving back with his parents, but he knew they would force him to attend synagogue and observe the Jewish feasts and festivals. He just couldn't handle that anymore.

One day Jonathan walked into a local coffee shop and met Avi. He didn't even realize that Dugit was run by messianic Jews as a city outreach. When Jonathan asked how much he owed for the coffee, Avi replied, "The coffee is on us. It's free."

"How about if I come back tomorrow? Is the coffee free again?"

"It is!" Avi smiled and added, "And it's free anytime you come by."

Jonathan enjoyed a week of free coffee, and then one day he started to read some of the literature at Dugit. He liked hanging out with the people who stopped in every afternoon. He was intrigued by the testimonies of young Jewish believers. All of them testified that Jesus had given them purpose in life and a new start. They talked about the freedom they now had in Christ. They shared how they also had the ability to forgive those who had hurt them. One man had lost his father in a suicide bombing in a city bus. The bitterness toward Palestinians that had controlled him was now gone.

Jonathan began to ask questions. Avi gave Jonathan a New Testament and told him that he might enjoy reading it. This

New Testament had the words that Jesus spoke printed in red. Avi playfully said, "Jonathan, you can read this, but I would stay away from the red letters. The words in red are Jesus' words; and since you come from an Orthodox background, I'm sure they will just make you angry. I think you should read the New Testament, but not the words in red. Remember—whatever you do, don't read the words in red!"

Jonathan went to his apartment that night and thought, *Why should I avoid Jesus' words? I can read them if I want to. I will read them!*

Jonathan stayed up that night and read only Jesus' words in all four Gospels. "I was overtaken by Jesus and how he answered tough questions. I was also drawn to him and the love that he extended to the worst of sinners. I had to know more about Jesus!"

Avi and Jonathan had a discussion about the Jewish Messiah. Avi's views were radically different, of course, than what Jonathan had been led to believe growing up. According to Orthodox Jews, the Messiah has not yet come; and Jesus is virtually ignored, even though he is considered a good rabbi by Orthodox rabbis. Avi gave Jonathan a list of one hundred prophecies from the Old Testament, paired up with a reference from the New Testament, and said, "Now read these prophecies from the Jewish Scriptures, and then see how they were fulfilled by Jesus in the New Testament. After that we can talk again."

The next afternoon Jonathan returned, as usual. He told Avi that he could see how the prophecies could be about Jesus.

"What are the chances that they could be fulfilled in just one man? Maybe Jesus *is* the Messiah."

Avi then asked a penetrating question. "Jonathan, you see how the Scriptures clearly point to Jesus as the Messiah, and you've felt him touch your heart as you read his words. What would it take for you to believe that Jesus is Lord and Savior?"

After thinking for a moment, Jonathan replied, "If Jesus could get me a job, I would know that he is Lord. Then I would believe."

"Would you receive him as your Savior if he got you a job?" Avi asked.

"I have been searching for a job for four months now. If Jesus is powerful enough to get me a job, then, yes, I would believe."

Avi said, "Great! Let's pray right now. Let's ask Jesus for a job for you. Let's ask him for one to turn up today."

Avi grabbed Jonathan's hand and prayed passionately. He began with a most familiar prayer for all Jews, called the Shema, from Deuteronomy 6, and then personalized it for Jonathan: "'Hear, O Israel: The LORD our God, the LORD is one. Love the LORD your God with all your heart and with all your soul and with all your strength.' Lord, Jonathan needs a job. But more important than that, he wants to believe that you love him, Jesus, and that you will supply all that he needs in life. Will you please get him a job?"

At that moment Jonathan's cell phone on the table in front of them began to ring. Jonathan looked up, and Avi told him to answer it.

"Jonathan turned pale white and looked at me with his mouth wide open and his eyes ready to pop out of his head," Avi recounts. "He was being offered a job over the phone right then, and they wanted him to start the next day!"

After Jonathan hung up, Avi hugged him and then asked, "Do you remember what you promised the Lord?"

Jonathan is just one of many Jews who have found Jesus in the last few years. I have a friend who moved to Israel in 1959. At that time he knew of only four Jews who believed that Jesus was the Messiah. Today that number is growing rapidly. When I began going to Israel in 1995, I remember wondering if there were any messianic believers in the country. There were, of course, but during the last thirteen years the number of Jews in Israel who are following Jesus as their Savior has risen steadily.

In his book *Epicenter*, Joel Rosenberg writes: "In 1967, when I was born, there were only five or six native Israeli believers in Jesus and fewer than 250 Jewish believers in Jesus in all of the Holy Land. Today there are more than 1,000 'sabra' believers— native-born Israeli Christians—and some 10,000 messianic Jews total in Israel. Worldwide in 1967, there were fewer than 2,000 Jewish followers of Jesus. Today conservative estimates say there are at least 100,000 Jewish believers, while some put the number at over 300,000."[6]

Rosenberg bases his numbers on personal interviews he has conducted in Israel. I have heard the same numbers while there. A man who prints Christian books in Hebrew estimates that

---

6. Joel C. Rosenberg, *Epicenter: Why the Current Rumblings in the Middle East Will Change Your Future* (Carol Stream, IL: Tyndale, 2006), 201.

there are over two hundred messianic congregations in Israel today.

Jewish Atheists

Even though the Holocaust ended over sixty years ago, Jewish survivors still live in Israel today. I have personally met a few of them, though they are a vanishing breed because of their age. The famous movie producer Steven Spielberg decided to capture their stories before it was too late. Since 1994 Spielberg's foundation has filmed nearly 52,000 Holocaust survivors and other witnesses in order to preserve their stories forever.[7]

These accounts will tear you apart. The word for the Holocaust in Hebrew is *shoah*. Perhaps no other event in Jewish history has shaped the modern nation of Israel more than this. Sadly, one theme is consistent throughout the interviews. Many of the survivors feared that someone was still looking for them in order to kill them simply for being Jewish.

Genocide is about the lowest level to which humanity can descend. This wasn't the only time the Jews were victims of such horror. They weren't even a nation yet the first time. About fifteen hundred years before Christ, Egypt, the world dominator of the day, attempted to kill all the Hebrew baby boys to control the population. Other nations, such as Assyria and Babylon, have followed suit.

Based on talks I have had with Holocaust survivors, I would say they are among the hardest Jews to reach with the gospel.

---

7. "Who We Are: History," University of Southern California Shoah Foundation Institute, http://college.usc.edu/vhi/history.php.

I'm sure that is in part because the people responsible for putting them in the death camps claimed to be Christians. They need love and compassion for all they have been through. In some cases these survivors lost every member of their families in the Holocaust.

During my talks with these survivors, I have discovered that some of them have given up their belief in God altogether and have become atheists. More than a few times I have heard the legitimate question, "If there is a God, where was he during World War II?" The depth of their pain causes them to conclude that there cannot be a God. If there was a God, he would have done something while one-third of the Jewish race was being destroyed. I cannot give them an answer for why the Holocaust happened, but I can give them hope.

I spoke with a woman in Tel Aviv who lost some of her family in the Auschwitz concentration camp. After she told me her story, our conversation turned to spiritual things. "Do you believe there is a God?" I asked.

"I can no longer believe there is a God in heaven," she responded. "That's a fairy tale."

"I'm sure that I can't even come close to feeling the pain that you feel in your heart for losing your family in the Holocaust," I said. "Your story is so sad, and I grieve with you and for you."

I went on to a different subject. At one point I asked, "Do you like the prime minister of Israel?"

"We are Jews, and we have the right to change our minds," she answered. "I like him today, but I probably won't like him tomorrow."

Later I said, "You know, I'm sure that many people thought the Jewish race might be wiped out completely during World War II. I would also bet most people never would have believed, in light of all the Jews were going through at the time, that in just a matter of three years they would be restored to their ancient homeland here in Israel. Do you think anyone would have been able to foresee that?"

"No!" she replied immediately.

"Neither do I," I continued. "So I can't answer the question of why God didn't stop the Holocaust. But just when it looked like the Jewish race would be annihilated, the war stopped; and months later Jews were streaming back into the land of Israel as a nation again. To me that is an amazing turnaround! And I cannot explain this turnaround apart from the existence of God. Can you?"

She thought for a few moments and then said, "You could be right . . . maybe."

Then I closed with this: "Remember, you're Jewish, and you have the right to change your mind. Maybe you'll rethink things today or tomorrow, and you'll give God an opportunity to be involved in your life again. And if you do, check out Jesus the Messiah. He is reaching out to you, and he loves you very much."

No matter how much I had prayed and tried to share Jesus with Holocaust survivors over the years, I had never heard of one of them coming to the Savior. That is, until this year. Four Holocaust survivors are known to have trusted Jesus the Jewish

Messiah and been born again in 2008. Their miraculous stories are significant breakthroughs in the Middle East.

Holocaust Survivors Meet Jesus

Isaac Cohen is one of those four Holocaust survivors. Isaac, or *Yitzhak*, as the name is pronounced in Hebrew, came to Israel when the nation was only a year old. In 1949 things were a lot different in Jerusalem. There was a freedom in the city that it is hard to find today. For the most part Arabs and Jews existed together, and in many cases they lived in the same neighborhoods. There were, of course, several wars in the last sixty years. But Isaac is a survivor, and his worst days in Israel have been a piece of cake compared to what he endured in Germany during World War II.

Isaac was twenty-four when he was liberated from Bergen-Belsen concentration camp in Germany. This infamous killing complex in Lower Saxony produced some chilling numbers. Between 1943 and 1945 an estimated 50,000 people died there. When Britain's 11th Armoured Division arrived at the scene on April 15, 1945, the findings were far worse than they had expected. More than 13,000 corpses in various stages of decomposition were strewn on the grounds unburied. Over 60,000 emaciated prisoners were found inside the camp, many of them seriously ill.[8]

---

8. "The 11th Armoured Division (Great Britain)," United States Holocaust Memorial Museum website, http://www.ushmm.org/wlc/article.php?lang=en&ModuleId=10006188.

Anne Frank is perhaps the most well-known Bergen-Belsen figure. During the two years her family was in hiding before being arrested and sent there, she kept a diary that later became the bestseller *Anne Frank: The Diary of a Young Girl*, which inspired the play and film titled *The Diary of Anne Frank*. The book has now been published in fifty languages. Anne and her sister died of typhus in Bergen-Belsen. It is estimated that as many as 35,000 in the camp died of this disease that is so prevalent during war and natural disasters.

When British soldiers arrived, they had to burn the camp to the ground in order to keep the typhus from becoming an epidemic. About 14,000 prisoners who were liberated and given medical care died soon afterward because they were too sick to survive. About 11,000 prisoners were put in a "displaced persons camp" that was established in German military barracks close to Bergen-Belsen.[9] Isaac was one of them.

Isaac survived the concentration camp because he was a young male and strong enough to help the German soldiers with daily chores. The work—burying bodies for ten hours a day—was grueling. Having this job kept the Germans from killing Isaac, but seeing thousands of innocent Jews killed and then haphazardly buried in shallow graves left him wondering if there could even be a God. This was so cruel. How could God let this happen?

Isaac held on to his Jewish heritage, but his religion didn't survive Bergen-Belsen. He left the displaced persons camp a practical atheist. Despite embracing secular humanism, Isaac

9. Ibid.

had a desire to live in Israel. He was given the chance in 1949, and he lived in Jerusalem ever since then. After settling in Israel, Isaac got married.

When Isaac turned eighty-four, he was no longer able to take care of himself. His wife had died, and they had no children. So Israel's government health program provided him nursing care in his home. Over the last few years Israel has allowed Filipinos to immigrate and join the work force. Two young Filipino women, both of whom were believers, were assigned to care for Isaac. Malea and Patricia soon began to love him like a father. He had so much wisdom. Isaac opened up to the two caretakers. Occasionally he would even talk about the horrors that he experienced those two years in Bergen-Belsen.

Two years later, in 2007, Isaac became ill and ended up bedridden. Now that he was immobile he often wanted company, so his nurses sat and talked with him for hours on end. One day, as the subject turned to spiritual issues, Isaac shared that with all the evil he had seen in his lifetime, he just couldn't fathom that there was a God. Yet he noticed joy in his two friends, and he was attracted to their zeal for life.

Malea told her story to Isaac over the next few hours. He listened intently and occasionally asked questions. Isaac so much wanted to know God, but the unresolved pain in his life was a formidable barrier. Malea sensed that great spiritual warfare was taking place. Patricia prayed intensely as she listened to the conversation. The women wondered if angels and demons were battling directly overhead.

In the end, the Spirit of God broke through. Isaac wept openly as decades of deep hurt came flowing out. After sobbing for several minutes, he invited Malea to lead him in a prayer to receive Jesus as his Savior. Malea and Patricia were crying and praising God as they prayed with Isaac. In the midst of his prayer to receive Jesus, Isaac's countenance changed as he was released from the pain he had carried for over sixty years.

Isaac was overjoyed. He hugged both of the women as tightly as his strength would allow, thanking them over and over. His smile was one of contentment and relief. Isaac surveyed the room slowly, smiled at Malea and Patricia, and looked toward the heavens. And then he died!

Malea recounts, "The smile was still on Isaac's face after he died. We called the paramedics; and when they arrived, they said, 'Look at his face. He died peacefully.' We were still crying and coming to grips with the miracle that God had done by saving Isaac's soul minutes before he faced eternity. Patricia looked at the paramedics and said, 'He was very peaceful. He was in perfect peace.'"

Isaac suffered greatly for no other reason than the fact that he was born Jewish. God must have a special love for his covenant people Israel, who have weathered so much throughout the ages. He orchestrated one last presentation of his offer of salvation to Isaac in the last moments of his life. The young Filipino women were responsive to the Spirit of God, who directed their words and their prayers. God meticulously wove everything together; and now Isaac is in heaven with his Savior, the Jewish Messiah.

Jesus was involved in his life all along. Isaac just didn't realize it until the last day of his earthly life.

Three other Holocaust survivors met Jesus in 2008. Like Isaac, all three died shortly after they received Christ as their Savior.

Rachel—Daughter of Jerusalem

Rachel Netanel has the gift of hospitality. How else can you explain that six nights of the week you can find her in her kitchen cooking for a group of people?

Rachel's family relocated from Morocco to Jerusalem shortly before she was born. Since they were Orthodox Jews, Rachel learned the Jewish Scriptures and the Jewish tradition all in one. For her the two were inseparable.

After getting married, Rachel lost interest in Judaism. Her husband was Orthodox, but his anger problem resulted in the end of their marriage. Rachel then became a policewoman, serving in Jerusalem for ten years. After that she studied fashion in Italy, and then she worked in Israeli television. When Rachel lost her job at the station, she felt like everything was lost. She had given up on her religion and her marriage, and now her job had given up on her.

During that low point in Rachel's life, God brought some messianic believers into her path. Over the following months Rachel became convinced that Yeshua was the Messiah and gave her heart to him. Her family, of course, was upset. They had survived all those years in Morocco as Jews living among Muslims. Who would have thought that Rachel, their only daughter born in Jerusalem, would disappoint the family and convert to Christianity? This was more than they could bear.

Rachel's great-grandfather, a highly respected scholar and rabbi, was a hero within Orthodox Judaism. He helped write the Jewish prayer book that is still used today by observant Jews. Rachel's family was like royalty in Israel. After she converted, they soon cut off their relationship with her altogether. Rachel was heartbroken but not defeated. She decided to reach out to others. She invites Jews (non-Orthodox Jews, that is, since Orthodox Jews wouldn't come) and Arabs into her home for dinner, and they willingly join her for her delicious Middle Eastern cuisine.

"It doesn't make a difference to me whether a person is Jewish, Muslim, or Christian," Rachel says. "I love them all, and I want them to know the truth. Arabs have been given a bad name by the press. The majority of them in Israel would choose to live here rather than any other place in the world." Many researchers would agree with Rachel. In a recent study done by Harvard's Center for Public Leadership, 76.9 percent of Arabs interviewed in Israel said that they would prefer to live in Israel rather than any other country.[10]

"The divisions between Muslims and Jews are not an issue when we are enjoying great food together around the table," Rachel observes. "Everything that I hope to bring to the

---

10. Todd Pittinsky, Jennifer Radcliff, and Laura Maruskin, "Coexistence in Israel: A National Study," Center for Public Leadership, Harvard Kennedy School, Harvard University, Cambridge, MA, 2008, 3, http://content.ksg. harvard.edu/leadership/images/CPLpdf/coexistence%20in%20israel.pdf.

people who visit my home is centered on Jesus, not religion or politics."

Rachel has led both Muslims and Jews to Jesus, and this hasn't set well with either group. She has had to move ten times and is routinely questioned by the police. Orthodox Jews call the authorities regularly to complain about Rachel's activities. The Orthodox have shunned her, threatened her, and spray-painted "Traitor" on her front door. They have even called Islamic leaders to complain that Rachel has been responsible for Muslims converting to Christianity!

Nevertheless, Rachel's home is a refuge to anyone who enters. She leads Bible studies each night after dinner. "I prefer to speak to people from the heart. I believe they can see my love and compassion for them and my willingness to serve them any way I can."

On Friday evenings Rachel celebrates the Sabbath by serving the traditional Sabbath dinner and reading and explaining Scripture, as is customary in Jewish homes. She lives near Jerusalem, in the town of Ein Kerem, which is believed to be the birthplace of John the Baptist. Many who live there today are involved in the New Age Movement.

"One of the most exciting things that we are doing now is having a worship time once a week on the Mount of Olives. Since it is in East Jerusalem, we have a large Arab group that comes and worships with us Jewish believers. This is the place where Jesus ascended to heaven, and one day he will return here also. How awesome it is to have Arab believers and Jewish believers praising Jesus together at this most important holy site. I know he smiles when we worship him here."

Rachel is one of the most engaging people I have ever met. How could anyone resist an invitation to her home? She also sponsors youth gatherings at the Dead Sea. The teenagers eat lots of food and act out stories from the Bible. "We have had several Israeli youth who are into the New Age give their lives to Christ as a result of 'Youth Night at the Dead Sea.' I can't afford it, but the Lord gets the money to me just in time to pay for the transportation and the food. We now have a new generation of young people in Israel who are passionate for Yeshua."

The night that Rachel told me her story there was a crowd of Orthodox Jews surrounding her home in Ein Kerem. They were shouting, "Get rid of her! She is converting Jews! We want her out of our neighborhood for good!"

"Rachel, how can you live like this?" I asked. "I don't know if there are more people in your house hearing about Jesus or more people outside your home protesting what you're doing! Is this normal for you?"

"Sure it is! The Orthodox were really mad when I had ten Arab workers remodeling my home in the midst of the Lebanese conflict in August of 2006. They thought it was awful that we were at war with Arabs and I was having them in for dinner and Bible study. But it didn't matter, because one of the workers came to faith in Christ and I baptized him in the bathtub that night! I invited the neighbors who were protesting to come watch the baptism, but they didn't show up. Personally, I think they are afraid of Jesus. But I will not give up. One day I will have the Orthodox Jewish community in my home for dinner. I can't wait to tell them about Jesus!"

When I was working on Rachel's story for this book, I e-mailed her to make sure I had all the details right. I also asked her how she was doing.

She wrote back and said that things were going just great. "God is doing so many wonderful things in my life and in the people he brings to me to tell them about him." Then she wrote that she had to go. The crowd picketing her home that night was rather large, and she needed to answer the door. The police were there again!

> *Blessed are you when men hate you, when*
> *they exclude you and insult you and reject*
> *your name as evil, because of the Son of Man.*
> *Rejoice in that day and leap for joy, because*
> *great is your reward in heaven. For that is how*
> *their fathers treated the prophets.*
>
> Jesus speaking in Luke 6:22–23

9

The Muslim Harvest in the Middle East

The Islamic cleric leaned into the camera and said, "A tragedy has happened: Muslims are converting to Christianity. Every year six million Muslims convert to Christianity."

I was in a home in Jordan with some pastors from around the Middle East, all of whom used to be Muslims themselves. They translated Sheikh Ahmad Al Qataani's words from Arabic to English for me as he spoke. The group fell silent as everyone was riveted to the sheik rattling off statistics on Al Jazeera, a popular Arabic satellite television channel in the Middle East. His disheartened look was replaced only by occasional outbursts of anger. Islam was losing people to Christianity—and losing them fast.

I remember thinking at the time how different this message was from what we often hear on the news. If you tune in to most of the media, you will come to the conclusion that there are hardly any Christians in the Middle East. And certainly no one would leave Islam for Christianity. Joel Rosenberg succinctly brings this false belief into the light:

> This Christianity-is-dying theme is complemented by the Islam-is-taking-over-the-world theme, so fashionable in academic and media circles over the past decade. In his 1996 book *The Clash of Civilizations and the Remaking of the World Order*, for example, Samuel P. Huntington argued that the percentage of Christians in the world will fall sharply in the twenty-first century and will be overtaken by the explosive growth of Muslims. . . . There is just one problem with such stories. They are not quite accurate. Not anymore at least."[1]

Why is this phenomenon of Muslims coming to Christ happening? How is it that we know there are believers in Jesus in the most unlikely places—like Mecca, Saudi Arabia, where it is illegal to be anything but a Muslim? How is it that the church in Tehran, Iran, is growing rapidly even though converting from Islam to Christianity in that country could get you thrown in jail or even killed?

The answer is that Muslims are falling in love with Jesus. It's as simple as that.

---

1. Joel C. Rosenberg, *Epicenter: Why the Current Rumblings in the Middle East Will Change Your Future* (Carol Stream, IL: Tyndale, 2006), 204.

Headline: Muslim Imam Becomes Christian Pastor

Can you imagine reading that headline in your local newspaper? That person certainly would have to have some incredible security protection. I can't think of a more serious offense in Islam than one of its studied and respected leaders defecting from the Muslim faith and becoming a leader in the Christian faith. But that is exactly what happened to Jihad Hamad.

When Jihad was forty years old, he preached his first sermon in a church outside of the Middle East. Stepping to the microphone to address this American congregation, he opened with these memorable words: "Twenty years ago I never would have been in this church. In fact, if I would have been in this church, I would have been figuring out a way to blow this place up, because I hated you with a passion. You Christians were at the top of my list of the people I despised the most. I was a fundamentalist Muslim. But I found Jesus—or, I should say, he found me."

What a way to begin a sermon! I looked at the crowd. Most of them had the kind of expressions on their faces that you might see in a theater during the latest Stephen King horror movie: eyes wide open and mouths in the same position. Jihad was there to tell the good news from the Middle East and to invite this congregation in New Mexico to pray for his work among Muslims. After that start, I can say that the people were all ears! But how did that transformation in Jihad's life take place?

Studying Islam as a teenager revolutionized Jihad's thinking. "For me, Islam was not merely a religion. It was an identity."

Like so many young Middle Eastern men, Jihad anticipated being part of the coming jihad—after which he was named—that would catapult Islam into world domination once more. He loved to read the history of the Islamic glory days during the beginning years of his religion.

Jihad was a leader in the Islamic fundamentalist movement in his Middle Eastern nation. He was known for his fierce determination to spread the religion of Islam globally. He had no time for the uncommitted Muslims he observed throughout his country. He hated them.

When he was old enough to serve in the military, Jihad joined the army. His heart was filled with pride every time he heard messages about the evils of Israel and the West. Jihad knew that he had found his calling. He continued his studies during his military service, eventually becoming an imam. He felt a sense of urgency to awaken fellow Muslims with the morning call to prayer. "I shouted, 'Prayer is better than sleep,' into the microphone each morning. I'm not sure that I even needed a microphone when it was my turn to rouse the troops!"

But along the way something changed for Jihad. "I love history, so on my days off I would dig deeply into the Hadith, which are the oral traditions of Muhammad's life, and into Islamic history. I started to become aware of how violent my religion was. I had become violent myself—unable to control my anger even toward the people I loved, like my family. I also began to have some doubts as I read conflicting passages in the Koran. And, finally, when the prophet Muhammad, whom I respected deeply, was asked about eternity, his answer paralyzed me with fear. In Sura 46:9 Muhammad replied, 'I do not know what will be done with me or with you.'

"How could I have missed that? I was shocked. How could I ever make it to paradise if my religion offered me no assurances? I sought answers to this question, and the response I received puzzled me even more: I was beaten! The imam I talked to made sure of it. I just wanted to find the truth; and I assumed that he, being a learned scholar, would help me. But he had no answer for me. So he beat me until I had no more questions."

When Jihad left the army, he also left Islam. He no longer went to the mosque. He stopped praying the five daily prayers. He even stopped fasting during the month of Ramadan. "My religious options were slim. I could not become a Jew, of course. That would be out of the question, even if I wanted to do so. I could not become a Christian either. So I became an atheist. I was finished with God and religion."

Jihad may have been right about "religion," but he was not finished with God. His life spiraled downward, as he got into drugs and alcohol to try to numb his pain. Jihad knew this wasn't the answer, but his anger was reaching new heights. He was angry at God. "Deep down inside I knew there was a God, but I thought that my ignoring him would teach him a lesson. Now that is arrogance, isn't it!"

About a year went by, and then a distant cousin of Jihad's named Mirna invited him to church. Since that was about the last place he wanted to spend a Sunday morning, he turned her down. But Mirna didn't give up; every week she invited Jihad to church. In order to get her off his back, he reluctantly agreed. "I will go once, but after that never ask me again!"

That Sunday the pastor's sermon title was "How You Can Know You Are Going to Heaven." His text was Jesus' words in John 14:6: "I am the way and the truth and the life. No one comes to the Father except through me."

"I knew that the God of the Bible the pastor was talking about was really God," says Jihad. "The pastor had prepared a message especially for me. His words spoke directly to the needs of my heart."

Mirna kept her word and never invited Jihad to go to church again. She didn't need to—he was there every Sunday on his own. "I wanted a relationship with God. I saw, through reading the Scriptures, that the Holy God of the Bible loved me. And furthermore, I could call him Father. He was my Father."

Jihad has given his life to reaching Muslims with the love of Christ. "The people of Islam are good people, not bad people. Sure, I have been persecuted by the extremists. But the average Muslim is so open to learning about God. They have so much to offer."

Jihad is right. He now pastors a church somewhere in the Middle East, and last year I visited this church with a team of believers from America. The church is composed of MBBs (Muslim-background believers). These former Muslims constitute one of the warmest and most loving groups of people I have ever encountered in the Middle East. The message we heard at their worship service, given that week by a visiting pastor, was biblical and convicting. The worship was from the heart; the room was emotionally charged as the people put everything they had into praising Jesus. Then, in my opinion, the best part happened. Jihad invited the believers to recite the memory verses of the week. One by one people rose and shared the entire second chapter of Acts—all forty-seven verses!

First, there was a thirty-nine-year-old woman who shared the verses beautifully while holding two babies. Next was a seventy-eight-year-old man. Then an eleven-year-old girl recited the chapter with emotion and hand gestures, like someone preaching a sermon. We Americans were amazed at the people's love for God and love for his Word. Most of them had been believers less than two years. Jihad has found many goodhearted Muslims looking for a personal relationship with the Father, just like he was.

The New Generation

"More Muslims have come to Christ in the past two decades than at any other time in history," David Garrison writes.[2] Fellow missionary Kevin Greeson adds:

> In North Africa, 50-60,000 Berber Muslims are now followers of Jesus Christ. A Turkic republic saw 4,000 Muslims come to know Jesus as Savior in one year. A mission group in India reported that they have seen an increase from three Muslim-background believers to 1,200 in only eight months. Another mission

---

2. David Garrison, *Church Planting Movements: How God Is Redeeming a Lost World* (Midlothian, VA: WIGTake Resources, 2004), 99.

effort working in North India is reporting 9,500 baptisms among Muslims in only four years. Over the past decade and a half, 13,000 Muslim Kazakhs have come to faith in Christ. Widespread reports of baptisms and new church starts are popping up all over the Muslim world. Nigeria reports several thousand baptized Muslim-background believers; Uzbekistan 80 new churches among Muslims; Tajikistan reports 15,000 Muslim converts; Afghanistan 3,000 secret believers; Iran over 800 baptisms of Muslims in one city alone.[3]

I believe I will see the Muslim world reached for Christ in my lifetime. That may sound unrealistic, but the new generation of believers in the Middle East today is bold and unafraid. They have resigned themselves to persecution.

An underground Bible college for former Muslims has a course aptly titled "What to Do When You Are Arrested for Your Faith." It is taught by a man who has been arrested several times. He begins the course by asking, "Are you willing to go to jail for Jesus?" He believes that the answer to this question is the determining factor of whether someone will be able to have a ministry among Muslims. And nobody drops out of his class. That's the new generation in the Middle East.

One young leader in Israel's West Bank says, "If you work in the Middle East and you want to bring Jesus to Muslims, fear cannot be a part of your vocabulary. If you live in fear, you cannot serve Christ here." I believe that to be true. That's why

---

3. Kevin Greeson, *The Camel: How Muslims Are Coming to Faith in Christ!* (Arkadelphia, AR: WIGTake Resources, 2007), 45.

I am thrilled and hopeful about the church in the Middle East. The "no fear" attitude is everywhere.

Phil Parshall, who has lived among and reached out to Muslims for decades, observes, "Muslims are wholeheartedly convinced they have found the truth. This strong, immovable conviction rode off into the deserts of Arabia on camels and horses in the mid-seventh century. It traversed mountains, crossed rivers, and pressed through the sand dunes of the Sahara. From the beginning Muslims believed that truth must be shared. Islam took its great commission seriously. Muslims lived and died for their faith."[4]

Can we, as believers, offer anything less to the people of Islam? Shouldn't we be willing to lay down our lives to bring the truth to them?

Many believers *are* willing to die in order to reach the Muslim world, and God is using their all-out commitment as in no other time in history. Today is the day for Muslims worldwide to hear about Jesus.

In the next chapter we will look at some areas of breakthrough. But before we do that, let's meet the most well-known evangelist to Muslims in the world today.

Zakaria Botross—Today's Apostle Paul to the Muslim World

Zakaria Botross is the most wanted man in the Middle East. In our travels in the region, we have heard of a price tag as

---

4. Phil Parshall, *The Cross and the Crescent: Understanding the Muslim Heart and Mind* (Waynesboro, GA: Authentic, 2002), 283–84.

high as twenty million dollars being on his head. What did he do to deserve this honor? He has led more Muslims to Christ than anyone in fourteen centuries of Islam. Zakaria Botross is a powerhouse when it comes to Muslim evangelism.

Raised in Egypt in the Coptic Orthodox Church, in the 1960s Zakaria became a priest. He was pious and a great student of the Bible, and he put his heart and soul into teaching church liturgy. Inside, though, Father Z was empty. So he began an all-out effort to know God personally. Through the writings of the early church father Cyril of Jerusalem, he came to the realization of the simplicity of the gospel. When he finally understood the enormity of what Christ had accomplished on the cross for him, he fell to his knees and was wonderfully converted.

Receiving God's grace and forgiveness for his sins, Zakaria became a new man. His life was transformed overnight. And so was his preaching. The Spirit of God was now on him. Zakaria prayed with passion; he laughed and he cried. He continued to research the subject of salvation, but now from the perspective of an insider and one who had been changed. The Holy Spirit began to work in his life so powerfully that Father Zakaria was now attracting crowds like never seen in the Coptic Church. Thousands came to hear him preach and join the revival. He was soon moved to St. Mark's Church in Cairo, the current seat of the Coptic Orthodox pope. The church began to soar, with attendance soon reaching the thousands, meeting not only on Sunday but two to three other times during the week.

St. Mark's became famous for two things. It was already re-nowned as the place where the remains of Mark the apostle and first missionary to Egypt were believed to be housed. But more importantly, now it became known as the place where God was. He was alive and setting people free from their sinful addictions and, in some cases, even demonization.

Zakaria, who was leading thousands of people to faith in Christ, eventually crossed the line. When Muslims began converting to Christ, the Coptic Church started to receive heavy pressure from Islamic leaders and the government of Egypt. Since Islam is the official religion of the country, conversion can result in persecution, imprisonment, or death. But none of that slowed Father Z down. He was on fire for Christ and unafraid.

Zakaria was not only being attacked by Muslims, but the Coptic Church jumped on the bandwagon and challenged his teaching. Under serious charges, he was removed from the church. His accusers claimed he was guilty of heresy, and he was removed from leadership until his trial. The church was in no hurry, scheduling the hearings for nine years later. Zakaria and his wife, Violet, were heartbroken. After ten amazing years in which the Holy Spirit so obviously had been validating this powerful ministry, the church was closed. Devastated, the people protested. But God had bigger plans for Zakaria and his family.

During this time, Zakaria was invited to debate Muslim scholars at a mosque on a Friday night. He was masterful. Using the Koran, he demonstrated Christian doctrines that Muslims reject, such as the Trinity and the deity of Christ. Humiliated, the scholars had only one way to fight back. They went to the government and accused Zakaria of the ultimate crime: evangelizing Muslims and inciting religious factionalism. Zakaria

Botross was tried, convicted, and sentenced to life in prison. The Islamic authorities thought they were rid of their nemesis, but they hadn't seen anything yet.

After months in jail, Zakaria amazingly was offered a deal. If he would agree to leave Egypt permanently, he was free to go. Father Zakaria and his family therefore left the country in which they had spent their whole lives and traveled to Australia. Was he now being silenced by the Muslims and the Coptic Church? He wanted to keep his family safe, but was his ministry to Muslims finished? He couldn't get out of his heart and mind the desire to reach people trapped in the religion of Islam.

When Zakaria's brother, Foad, was a young man, he developed a personal relationship with the Lord and a ministry to Muslims. He eventually was targeted by Muslim extremists. One night a large group of men abducted Foad, cut out his tongue, and brutally murdered him. Zakaria was given Foad's Bible. The blood of his brother who was martyred watered a seed planted within Zakaria that would determine the course of his life. Foad's life would not be lived in vain, and neither would Zakaria's. Even if the Muslims killed them both, he would fight for his faith—even unto death.

Father Z turned seventy years old. Most of his friends were retired from ministry at that age. He was also thousands of miles from the Middle East. Despite the passion in his heart, his vision to reach Muslims seemed unrealistic. But then one of Zakaria's friends had a brilliant idea: the Internet would be a great way to get the gospel to Muslims. In 1999, Father Z began an Internet chat room on Paltalk.com. Muslims began logging on and asking questions about the Bible and the Koran. Some were open and had honest doubts about Islam; others wanted to argue. Zakaria was ready for both. He responded to the following objections to Christianity frequently expressed by Muslims:

- *The Trinity*—Muslims believe that Christianity teaches that God the Father had a physical relationship with God the mother Mary. Not only is this inaccurate, but it is offensive to Christians. Zakaria demonstrated from the Scriptures that the Trinity is revealed in the deeds of the Father (Romans 1:18–20), Son (Hebrews 1:1–4), and Holy Spirit (Psalm 104:30). He also dispelled the error that Mary was part of the Trinity.

- *The deity of Christ*—Muslims believe that only God can give life, answer prayer, and provide for our daily needs. Yet Jesus did all of this, as seen in John 11:38–44; John 15:7, 16; and Mark 8:1–9.

- *The crucifixion of Christ*—Islam teaches that Judas actually died on the cross, while the disciples were confused and later claimed that Jesus was crucified. But as we see in Scriptures like Hebrews 9:11–14, that would have destroyed Jesus' reason for coming to earth.

- *The inspiration of Scripture*—Muslims believe that the Bible is not inspired, yet Muhammad claimed that it was in Sura 2:89 and Sura 5:46.

- *The Gospel of Barnabas*—This book, purporting to be a depiction of the life of Jesus written by the apostle Barnabas, mentions Muhammad as a prophet and is a favorite of Muslim scholars. Yet it has been proved to have been fraudulently composed in the fifteenth or sixteenth century.

- *The supposed mention of Muhammad in the Bible*—In John 14, Jesus spoke of the Holy Spirit as Counselor or Comforter, using the Greek word *paraclete*. Muslims changed the word to *periclyte*, which means "famous or praised one." Muslims claim this is a title for Muhammad. Zakaria showed that the context of this passage is impossible to apply to Muhammad.

- *Perceived contradictions in the Bible*—These arguments arise from an incomplete understanding of the text, the context, and biblical inspiration. Father Z answered these objections one by one.

Zakaria was easily able to disarm each argument. Soon the Internet site was overwhelmed, and there was a need to expand the ministry. In 2003 his team decided to produce twenty programs for TV, and they have not stopped filming since. The Al-Hayat network beams programs to the Middle East every day of the week. *Al-Hayat* means "life," and that's what Zakaria is bringing to the Middle East.

The program is one of the most watched programs in the Middle East. Zakaria's ministry believes that twenty million viewers tune in each month to hear the good news and listen to Father Zakaria dispel the false claims of Islam. The ministry's website, www.islam-christianity.net, also registers seven million website hits per month, as reported in the book *Defying Death: Zakaria Botross—Apostle to Islam.*

Zakaria pulls no punches. He says over the air, "Christianity begins with God becoming incarnate in Jesus. Islam begins with Satan becoming incarnate in Muhammad." It's easy to see why Zakaria has so many enemies!

Father Z is answering questions that Muslims have wrestled with for centuries. They can have their questions answered in the privacy of their home. The staff follows up new believers via the Internet. The ministry is continually buried under requests for more discipleship materials. Zakaria defends the Christian faith and points out the numerous errors in the Koran and the Hadith, the supposed sayings of Muhammad.

While I was having lunch with Zakaria recently, he said, "Tom, did you know that in the Koran and Hadith there are 35,000 references to war and jihad and 10,000 references to sex?" Father Z is a walking encyclopedia!

In twenty-five years of ministry in Egypt, Zakaria saw about five hundred Muslims come to Christ. Since he has been on the Internet and TV, Father Z and his team have corresponded with over one million people who have left Islam to follow Jesus as Savior! Only God could orchestrate that. And all of this has occurred after Zakaria's seventieth birthday!

Zakaria Botross now lives in an undisclosed location. Islamic leaders cannot defeat him, and that's why they want him dead. Despite the threats and constant danger, Father Z has a great love for the Muslims of the world. He believes that the majority of them are good people who simply have been deceived by their leaders. Their hearts are generally open, and he has been called to reach them with the love of Christ.

Zakaria's birth name was Feyez. Upon entering the ministry, he adopted the name Zakaria—from the biblical prophet Zechariah. His life verse couldn't describe him any better:

> *"Not by might nor by power, but by my Spirit,"*
> *says the LORD Almighty.*

Zechariah 4:6

10

Significant Breakthroughs in the Islamic World

The church in the Muslim Middle East today is empowered by God and serving faithfully in the core of the world's spiritual conflict. In the last few decades that spiritual warfare has increased exponentially. But the church is strong and vibrant. Three characteristics jump out when you spend time with churches in the midst of the Muslim world. And each of these characteristics is essential for a church to make an effective impact on its culture—whether that church is in Iran or England.

The Church in the Middle East Is a Worshiping and Praying Church.

The church in the Middle East does less and worships more. Hours and hours are devoted to worshiping the Father and interceding for believers around the world. The first time I went to Iran a leading pastor said to me, "Tom, I have a message for the American church. Tell them the believers in Iran pray for them every day!" That brings tears to the eyes of Christians in the United States. Most of us didn't even know there were believers in Iran. If you get your worldview from cable news, you probably think that all Iranians hate Americans and want to wipe them out.

The churches in Iran worship and pray intensely. They meet several times a week, during the night for security reasons. The typical church meeting lasts from midnight till 5:00 a.m.

In her book *Having a Mary Heart in a Martha World*, Joanna Weaver writes, "When we put work *before* worship, we put the cart before the horse. The cart is important; so is the horse. Put the horse first, or we end up pulling the cart by ourselves. Frustrated and weary, we can nearly break under the pressure of service, for there is always something more that needs to be done."[1] The church in the Muslim world has the horse before the cart. I have never seen such a spiritual appetite in my thirty-two years of ministry. No wonder these believers are making such a difference. No wonder God is moving in power.

The Church in the Middle East Is a Persecuted Church.

In the last few years important spiritual leaders in the Middle East have been martyred for Christ. As sad as this is for their families, not one of these lives has been wasted. In fact, God's

---

1. Joanna Weaver, *Having a Mary Heart in a Martha World: Finding Intimacy with God in the Busyness of Life* (Colorado Springs: WaterBrook Press, 2000), 10 (italics in original).

sovereign timing has used each death to catapult the church into a new level of authority within its nation.

For years the believers in the Gaza Strip have met the needs of the people living there. When Rami Ayyad, a leader of the Bible society, was brutally murdered, moderate Muslims took note and reached out to the believers with acts of kindness. This broke new ground within Gaza. Muslims know the believers are under scrutiny, threat, and endless persecution. Yet that has never stopped them from helping needy Muslims. These frontline saints risk everything to serve.

Rami's death proved that there are moderate Muslims in Gaza. It also proved that Hamas' vise grip on the people is backfiring. The people despise the new regime that was supposed to liberate Gaza. Goodhearted Muslims know that a senior member of Hamas was responsible for killing Rami. They want their voices to be made known in Gaza. Both Muslims and believers have to live under Hamas' corrupt and brutal rule. Rami's death has opened doors for the believers into the lives of Muslims. God has used Rami in death even more than in life.

That's what Jesus does with his church. When believers suffer, the church grows. But followers of Christ have to be willing to embrace suffering. When I am with believers in Gaza, Iran, Syria, or the West Bank, the prayer I hear most often is, "Lord, please don't take away the persecution—but use us in the midst of it!" I don't know about you; but when I have faced difficulty, my first prayer is for God to get me out of it as fast as possible. That proves, however, that my prayers are centered on my desires rather than God's. What's more important—my comfort or his eternal plan? I've just convicted myself!

The Church in the Middle East Is a Unified Church.

The church in the Muslim Middle East understands unity. Without it they rapidly would be buried in defeat.

In Ephesians 4:11–13, Paul instructs the church on spiritual gifts: "It was [Christ] who gave some to be apostles, some to be prophets, some to be evangelists, and some to be pastors and teachers, to prepare God's people for works of service, so that the body of Christ may be built up until we all reach unity in the faith and in the knowledge of the Son of God and become mature, attaining to the whole measure of the fullness of Christ." Unity becomes a byproduct of believers living out their giftedness.

The church in the Middle East has a maturity well beyond its years. Christians there don't get caught up in petty squabbles, because the stakes are much higher. They have a clear and dangerous mission, and every believer is critical in order for the body to be successful in fulfilling the Great Commission. Ministries work together. Denominations don't get hung up on their differences. All efforts are maximized for the glory of God.

Some Breakthrough Nations

Syria

In the first few centuries of the church's existence the area of Syria was a robust outpost for the cause of Christ. A few centuries later, however, it became a hotbed of Islamic fanaticism. Damascus,

Significant Breakthroughs in the Islamic World

the ancient city of the Bible, became an integral part of the Islamic world through the Umayyad dynasty centered in the Syrian capital city. Because of the harsh leadership of the Assad family in recent decades, the church has been quiet and fairly nonevangelistic. The current ruler, Bashar al-Assad, and his predecessor and father, Hafez al-Assad, are members of the Alawite religion. The Alawites are a splinter group from Islam; some Muslims consider Alawites a part of Islam, and others do not.

In 2007 the first church made up of Alawites was planted in Syria. Because of their religion's secretive approach to faith, Alawites are starving for a personal relationship with God. Jesus, of course, offers this; and significant numbers of Alawites are now interested in the gospel.

Syria has a large deaf population. They generally have been ignored by the majority Sunnis and the other Muslim sects. One man's determination to train some of his deaf friends with the EvangeCube has resulted in an all-deaf church in Syria. These believers have a vision to reach out to the many deaf people in the nation.

Whenever Americans connect with the church in Syria, the heat is turned up on believers immediately. We have come to expect the secret police to be "with us" wherever we go. A seasoned leader got so tired of the secret police showing up at every church we visited that he decided to go on the offensive. Seeing the same policemen for many years, he became familiar with them and even got to know them by name. One day he called the police headquarters in his city and talked to a man whom I will call Abdullah. He said, "You know that I have American friends here, and we see you following us everywhere. Tonight we are driving an hour to meet with a church, and I'm sure you already know about it and will arrive about the same time we do. Why don't you save the gasoline and just ride with us? We'd be glad to have you come with us."

After a long silence, Abdullah accepted the invitation. When we picked him up, he didn't look sinister. In fact, he was quite nice and respectful. He's a human being just doing his job, right?

During the EvangeCube training, we noticed that the pastor of the church gave Abdullah an EvangeCube as he passed them out to the congregation. The training takes a few hours, and during that time we noticed that Abdullah couldn't take his eyes off the cube. He learned how to turn it from start to finish, never once looking up at us.

At the end of the training session we always make sure the attendees present have the opportunity to pray to receive Christ, just in case this is the first time the gospel makes sense to them. We asked all of them to bow their heads, and we explained the gospel one more time. Then we invited them to repent and pray so that they could become a child of God. When we finished, we noticed Abdullah in the corner of the room, with tears streaming down his cheeks. He accepted Christ that night! The ride home was one of tears and laughter and singing. I learned a great lesson that night: no one is unreachable—no one.

Abdullah is growing in his faith in Jesus Christ now, and his smile is contagious. All it took was an invitation from a bold leader who was willing to risk a call to the secret police. It could have resulted in endless questioning for this Syrian believer, and perhaps, even in him getting thrown in jail. But it was worth it, because this secret policeman will be in heaven one day.

The body of Christ in Syria is filled with joy and is hopeful about its future.

Israel's West Bank

I've never enjoyed watching grown men fight, especially when they are Christians. But that's what you often see when you go to the Church of the Holy Sepulchre in Jerusalem, which commemorates the greatest miracle of all time—Jesus' resurrection. Six Christian denominations share the custodianship of the traditional location of the crucifixion and empty tomb: Eastern Orthodox, Roman Catholic, Armenian, Ethiopian Orthodox, Syrian Orthodox, and Egyptian Coptic Orthodox.[2] And here is where the fighting comes in. Unfortunately, the six denominations are continually at each other's throats.

I will never forget the first time I visited the church, in 1995. As we walked in the front door, we were greeted by an Eastern Orthodox priest and a Syrian Orthodox priest in the midst of a brawl. I hadn't seen this kind of fistfight since my junior high days! What made the scene even sadder was the fact that a large crowd was watching and that television cameras were rolling. The fight, it turns out, was over an extension cord in the Syrian section that had somehow crossed the dividing line and was partially resting in the Eastern Orthodox section. No

---

2. Etty Boochny, *The Holy Land: Follow the Steps of Jesus* (Bnei Brak, Israel: Steimatzky Books, 2005), 148.

wonder the church has had difficulty reaching Muslims in the Middle East!

Two brothers, Omar and Muhammad, are members of the Muslim family that opens and locks the front door of the Church of the Holy Sepulchre each day. It has been this way since Saladin, the Arab conqueror, wrested control of Jerusalem from the crusaders in 1187. Saladin gave the keys to two Muslim families in order to keep the peace at this Christian holy site.

Christian denominations like the ones that control the Church of the Holy Sepulchre in Jerusalem are dying in the Middle East. Their members are getting old, and many of their more nominal members are moving out of the region altogether. Persecution has usually caused nominal Christians to flee or, in some cases, even to convert to Islam. But the new generation of churches is different. They are filled with young people who are vibrant in their faith. These Arab believers know that living in the shadow of Islamic fanaticism means they will never have a normal life, but they have counted the cost.

In the West Bank, food distribution teams take necessary staples into places like Ramallah, Jenin, Salfit, and Jericho. Medicine is also dispensed, as the needs are enormous among the Palestinians. Several Christian groups have answered the call to bring the love of Christ to Muslims in the West Bank.

I have had the privilege on a few occasions to take boxes of food and medicine into homes in Ramallah. Listening to the suffering families' stories was almost unbearable. One woman lost her husband in a shoot-out between the Palestinian Authority and Hamas. She had five children and no job. The food we gave her would feed her family for a month. Tears ran down her cheeks as she asked us to pray for her and her family.

The Palestinian believers prayed with such fervency and intensity that the sweet Muslim woman began to weep openly. "I have never heard praying like that in my life! You have such a love for God that it just filled this house. Would you come back and pray with me again?"

The team did return, and the woman began to open up about her dissatisfaction with the continual war against Israel. She believes that it has done nothing to help the Palestinians in the long run, but she had been afraid to talk about her views. She just wanted some friends.

One day a relief team went in and fed about twenty-five families. Eighteen people prayed to receive Christ that day! That night all of them received their first discipleship lesson on how to walk with Christ.

Palestinian believers are meeting needs in the midst of the West Bank conflict—and in the process are seeing Muslims turn to Jesus and new churches form.

Jordan

The Jordanians call themselves "the sweet Arabs." This is one fun-loving group of people! Prayer meetings extend into all hours of the night. The believers worship with all their heart. And they are some of the most effective evangelists in the Middle East, starting about seventy new churches in 2007. God is knocking down barriers in Jordan, and the various Christian ministries there have a simple but effective plan to spread the gospel. Here are the basics:

- The ministries stay connected and work together to accomplish the same goals. This sounds good to those of us in the West, but the Jordanians actually practice this philosophy!

- Jordanian believers have a heart for the people who live in all the villages throughout Jordan. There are about a thousand villages, and not one of them is overlooked by the ministries during outreach campaigns. This is tough, since these rural and less-educated Muslims tend to be more fanatical. The believers may have to visit villages several times before anything significant happens. The people in one village threw stones at the believers five times before they were finally able to enter. Though the fundamentalists tried to kill them, they hung in there; and now a church has been planted in the remote village.

- Because Jordan has a significant tourist industry, it's easy for mission teams to get into the country to help out the national leaders. Christians are able to bring helpful resources with them into Jordan. And in some cases the churches are producing resources themselves.

- The believers move forward in prayer. This is the foundation for all the Christian ministries. The believers know how to pray, and they devote many hours to doing so.

- Evangelism is for every believer. New believers learn to share their faith from day one. Our e3 ministry has been blessed to train at least 1,500 believers with

the EvangeCube in Jordan. And we are just one of
the many ministries that are equipping believers with
evangelistic tools.

- Jordan is a stopover for many refugees from various
  Middle East wars. The believers take advantage of this
  opportunity to meet needs and share the gospel. They
  have been responsible, for example, for starting at least
  thirty churches in Iraq. As refugees gather in Amman
  and other cities in Jordan, the Jordanian Christians
  reach out to them with great results.

In 2002 e3 Partners had the privilege of working with ten
Iraqi churches in Jordan. All of these Iraqi believers planned to
return to their country. When I went to Iraq in 2003, we met
many of those same believers. The believers in Jordan had led
them to Christ, discipled them, and helped them form a new
church while they were still in Jordan. By the time they returned
to Iraq, the churches were already established and had trained
leadership. They were mature, focused, and had a vision to reach
their own country.

Iraq

The Iraqi believers have needed every ounce of maturity
they gained while living in Jordan. Upon returning to their
homeland, they have found themselves in the midst of a bloody
Sunni-Shiite war. They have suffered intense persecution as each
group tries to hold on to its turf in the post-Saddam days. Both
sects of Islam are filled with hatred for Christians.

The worst thing you can be accused of in Iraq is being "pro-
American." Christians are given that label as they are supposedly

a part of the "religion of the West." Christianity, of course, is from the East; but there is no reasoning with jihadists. This type of propaganda goes virtually unchallenged in places like Iraq. Islamic clerics have a hard time convincing others of their ideology. Therefore, like some of the worst dictators in history, they use threats and brainwashing. Baghdad has experienced growth in its churches, but the relentless persecution has caused some of the believers to leave the capital city of Iraq.

The Kurds, in northern Iraq, are the most open to the gospel today. Kurdistan is an area about the size of the state of Nebraska. Spanning across the mountainous region of southwest Asia, it also includes parts of southeast Turkey and northwest Iran. The Kurds are the fourth-largest ethnic group in the Middle East, after the Arabs, Iranians, and Turks.

Saddam Hussein waged the genocidal Anfal Campaign against the Kurds in the late 1980s. Saddam ordered massacres against the Kurds, forcing many to relocate. The chemical bomb attacks were meant to eradicate every Kurd inside of Iraq. Estimates of the number of Kurds who were murdered range from 100,000 to more than 200,000. Saddam launched "gendercide," as he attempted to kill every male of military age.

The Kurds in Iraq have been to hell and back. When Saddam was about to be attacked by the coalition forces in 2003, he offered the Kurds a deal. He would give them the northern half of Iraq if they joined the fight against the infidels. The Kurds said, "No way!"

Today the Kurdish section of Iraq is the most stable region in the whole country. The Kurds are enjoying their newfound autonomy. Tourism is even streaming into the area. The Kurds are Sunni Muslims; but after experiencing such horrific treatment from other Muslims, they have opened up to the gospel.

One Middle East evangelist believes that the Kurdish church will soon be the strongest in the entire region. Saddam wanted to gas the Kurds and rid Iraq of them. Now he is gone, and the people are thriving and finding true freedom in Jesus Christ. They were victims of genocide, but now they are a part of one of the biggest revivals in the Middle East in decades. God has brought the Kurds back from the grave.

The church in the Middle East is strong and healthy despite the considerable odds it faces. Some forces within the religion of Islam are pursuing jihad and a plan to dominate the world through control and intimidation. The vast majority, however, are fed up with what Islam has done to their lives, their families, their country, and their region. They have given up on their religion and are Muslim in name only. Others are breaking free altogether and finding Jesus Christ as the Savior who loves them. Unconditional love is powerful in the life of a Muslim. No longer are these new believers following the slavish demands of a harsh and condemning God. They are now following the true God, who draws near to them with the tenderness and affection of a loving Father.

The Dividing Line

The Western world changed on September 11, 2001. But the world of Islam may have changed more. A dividing line was drawn. Most of the Islamic world felt shame and dishonor for the actions that led to the deaths of nearly three thousand people. Of course, jihadists were celebrating the significant impact made upon "the great Satan." But the average Muslim was not. In extensive interviews throughout the Middle East, we continually hear that over half of Muslims worldwide are not practicing their faith whatsoever.

Muslims are born into their religion and do not choose it like born-again Christians do. Therefore a significant number of people within Islam have little investment in it. They have not considered whether it is the right religion. They have not investigated other religions. They have been taught how to think. But there is something deep inside every heart that will often derail the control that Islam seeks to have over people. It's called sin. The human heart is rebellious; so while parents try to force their children to be a certain way and to think like them, it doesn't always work.

You can clearly see that in the young people in the Middle East today. The Muslim culture is a youth-oriented culture. For example, in the Gaza Strip the median age is around fifteen.[3] True, the militant Muslim leadership is directing these young people into the path of jihad. Some are willing to go this way. Some are forced to go this way. Some are going in the opposite direction altogether.

In Syria the majority of young people dress in very modern clothes. Youth are more concerned about being "hip" than about looking like committed Muslims. It is shocking to see how some

---

3. Mark Steyn, *America Alone: The End of the World as We Know It* (Washington DC: Regnery Publishing, 2006), xvii.

young men and women in Damascus dress. I imagined that all the young women would be in burqas and traditional garb. Not so. And same for the guys. The traditional Islamic dress for men is the simple white gown with sandals and an Islamic skullcap, called a kufi. There are some young men who dress that way, but not many in the capital city.

In Iran drugs are plentiful and parties are nightly. Young people are depressed and searching. Suicide is a major problem among the youth in Iran. While talking to a Muslim man in Iran, I said, "You must think America is awful, with all the sex in movies and the anything-goes philosophy."

He replied, "Tom, we have everything going on in Iran that you do in America. We just don't boast about it and put it on television." I have found that to be true. Sin is sin. And it is a global problem, not just an America problem.

The control of women is much stronger in Iran than in Syria. Sharia law has seen to that. Although most Muslim nations incorporate aspects of Sharia law into their constitution, Iran and Saudi Arabia are the two countries that claim to implement Sharia law fully into all areas of life.

In Iran the mullahs, the clerics with national position, are considered the ultimate authority. In Saudi Arabia the Koran is considered to be the constitution, and it has the ultimate authority. It still comes down to interpretation of the Koran. In Iran and Saudi Arabia the women are veiled in fulfillment of Sharia law. But they wear very fashionable veils and expensive clothes. They look like something out of Beverly Hills. And when you fly out of Iran, the pilot at some point announces, "We are now out of Iranian airspace." As soon as he makes that announcement, the veils and burqas come off so fast it reminds me of graduation at the Air Force Academy when the cadets throw their hats in the air to celebrate!

So most young people in the Middle East don't want to grow up and live like traditional Muslims. They don't follow the religion closely, and they don't conform to its dress code. Even though they are forced to act and dress a certain way in Sharia law countries, they still push the limits to the extreme. When Muhammad required women to be veiled, I'm not sure he had in mind that the women of Iran and Saudi Arabia would look like something out of a Nordstrom catalog. But who could blame them? Every woman wants to be attractive. But no matter the religion, there are always loopholes with the law.

And the majority of young people in the Middle East don't think like traditional Muslims. There is a strong desire not to be isolated from the West. Youth know that if they live in a country known for Islamic fanaticism they will have fewer options in life. In Iran, young men openly told me how they hated serving in the military. But they had no other choice. To make sure no one slips through the cracks, they cannot receive a driver's license until they serve in the Islamic Republic Army.

After 9/11, Muslims worldwide began to ask questions like "Do I have to be a terrorist to be a good Muslim?" "Is my goal in life to rule the world, or do I just want to practice my religion?" "Will I have to live the rest of my life in the midst of war because Islamic leadership will have it no other way?"

All of these questions, combined with genuine apathy toward Islam, are great signs for the gospel. If 10 percent of Muslims are considered hard-line and fundamentalist, then approximately 100 million Muslims are more than enough to wage an effective jihad against the rest of the world. If 50 percent of Muslims are not practicing Islam (and this number may be low), then the door is wide open, and today is the day for the church to make a major effort to reach the Muslim world. The young people are rapidly turning away from Islam as their parents practiced it, and they are reachable.

Hope in the Power of God

Can you imagine a Middle East where there are churches in every village, Bibles for every new convert, godly leadership in place to serve, and a revival that no one can deny? Can you see families that are happy and marriages that are based on biblical principles and guided by the love of Christ? How different this would be for a religion that in essence values men above women.

What would it look like for a generation of children to be raised in a home where they learned of Jesus' love and forgiveness at an early age? What if young people lived in a peaceful region, where suicide bombings were a thing of the past? What if the Middle East became known for people who had the ability to forgive instead of for people who continued to build on strongholds of bitterness?

How about this? What if the church in the Middle East was so strong and attractive that it began to send missionaries to the rest of the world? The oldest feud on the planet is between Isaac and Ishmael. What if, with the church leading the way, their descendants forgave each other and generations of hatred and bitterness evaporated for the world to see? Can you imagine if the original Hatfields and McCoys patched it up for good? That would do more for world peace than any UN resolution or peace agreement between governments.

Those of us who serve Christ in the Middle East live for that day. Is there any chance of all this happening? Yes, because the power of almighty God has no limits. More than anyone, we believers are the people inspired and driven by hope. We have seen the hope that Jesus brings to people living in the worst imaginable conditions. In the midst of it they have joy in their hearts and smiles on their faces. We have seen Jesus transform a village, and that could easily spread like a fire throughout the Middle East and then to the world.

Does Jesus have one last revival planned for the world before he returns? Those who labor for Christ in the bull's-eye of today's spiritual war believe he does.

I have great hope for the Middle East for three reasons. The first is because . . .

The Power of God Is Unlimited!

The Old Testament prophet Daniel faced the challenge of his lifetime. King Darius ruled the vast Medo-Persian Empire.[4]

---

4. I realize there is a great deal of mystery and scholarly debate about the identity of the king named Darius in Daniel. But for the purposes of this book I am simply taking the Book of Daniel at face value and referring to this king as "Darius."

When his administrators came and suggested thirty days of prayers directed toward the king himself, it was something his royal ego just couldn't turn down. And since he issued the edict "in accordance with the laws of the Medes and Persians," it was irreversible.

King Darius had pride, but he still had a heart. He was shocked when he heard that the first violator of the law he had signed into existence was Daniel. Darius had great respect for Daniel. After all, he had appointed him one of his three top administrators and was planning to elevate him over the whole kingdom. But it was too late. Daniel was thrown to the hungry lions one night, and the king spent that horrible night without food, sleep, or the usual royal entertainment.

When Darius rushed to the den in the morning, he was amazed to find Daniel alive. The lions hadn't even scratched him! What happened next is astonishing, considering that we're talking about a pagan king.

> Then King Darius wrote to all the peoples, nations and men of every language throughout the land:
>
> "May you prosper greatly! I issue a decree that in every part of my kingdom people must fear and reverence the God of Daniel. For he is the living God and he endures forever; his kingdom will not be destroyed, his dominion will never end. He rescues and he saves; he performs signs and wonders in the heavens and on the earth. He has rescued Daniel from the power of the lions."
>
> So Daniel prospered during the reign of Darius and

the reign of Cyrus the Persian. (Daniel 6:25–28)[5]

Darius saw the power of the living God, and then this pagan king wrote these words of truth about him—words that God chose to include in his Word forever. In an instant this egomaniacal ruler believed that *God's* kingdom was enduring, in contrast to *his* kingdom, which was destined to fade one day.

I have hope in my heart today, and it's not because I'm getting my worldview from cable news. *I have hope because the power of God is unlimited!* Proverbs says that the king's heart is in the hand of the Lord (Proverbs 21:1). And God can direct it just like he does a stream. He could change the heart of Mahmoud Ahmadinejad. He could capture the heart of the ayatollah of Iran and transform him too. I'm not saying that Darius repented and became a follower of the God of Israel, but he did humble himself and give praise and honor to him. He also announced this to his entire kingdom.

We need aggressive prayer for the leaders of the Islamic nations. We need intercession for these nations that are held in bondage. In one Middle East country the believers called a forty-day prayer and fasting initiative. They prayed that God would unlock the chains binding their nation, starting with the government. In their prayers they targeted the top forty hard-line leaders in the country. They prayed that the leaders would repent

---

5. I realize that the NIV text note on Daniel 6:28 states that "So Daniel prospered during the reign of Darius and the reign of Cyrus the Persian" could be read "So Daniel prospered during the reign of Darius, that is, the reign of Cyrus the Persian."

and come to Christ; and if that didn't happen, they prayed that God would do whatever necessary to remove them from power.

These believers could pray that way with full confidence, because the power of God is unlimited.

The second reason I have hope for the Middle East is because . . .

The Plan of God Is Unending!

All of the talk about nuclear war, jihad, and an Islamic takeover of the world is no surprise to the God of heaven. He isn't biting his fingernails, trying to figure out what to do next! His plan continues. The first chapter of the Book of Ezra tells us that Cyrus, the king of the Medo-Persian Empire, fulfilled the word that God had spoken through the prophet Jeremiah and permitted the Jews to go back to their homeland.[6] In fact, he *encouraged* them to return and rebuild the temple and even helped make that possible.

> In the first year of Cyrus king of Persia, in order to fulfill the word of the LORD spoken by Jeremiah, the LORD moved the heart of Cyrus king of Persia to make a proclamation throughout his realm and to put it in writing:
>
> "This is what Cyrus king of Persia says:
>
> "'The LORD, the God of heaven, has given me all the kingdoms of the earth and he has appointed me to

---

6. I realize that many scholars feel that "Darius" and "Cyrus" are different names for the same person. But, again, for the purposes of this book I am taking the biblical record at face value and treating them as two separate kings.

build a temple for him at Jerusalem in Judah. Anyone of his people among you—may his God be with him, and let him go up to Jerusalem in Judah and build the temple of the LORD, the God of Israel, the God who is in Jerusalem. And the people of any place where survivors may now be living are to provide him with silver and gold, with goods and livestock, and with freewill offerings for the temple of God in Jerusalem.'" (Ezra 1:1–4)

The God in heaven again "moved the heart" of a king. Cyrus was another ego-driven monarch. In 1879 an ancient Babylonian cylinder was unearthed in Iraq, and archaeologists named it the "Cyrus Cylinder," as this same Cyrus recorded his "charter of human rights" on it. This king never minced words when talking about himself. I saw a replica of the famous cylinder in a museum in Iran. It starts like this: "I am Cyrus, king of the world, great king, legitimate king, king of Babylon . . ." and on and on and on. You get the idea. Another king who sounds like an NBA basketball player talking about himself in an interview.

What a turnaround! King number two? No problem for almighty God. Putty in his hands. Cyrus sent the Jews back to Israel to rebuild their temple, and he even helped pick up the tab! The plan of God is unending, so it didn't matter if the king in power was a jerk, a pagan, or Public Enemy Number One. God had plans, and no one got in the way of them—not even the ruler of "all the kingdoms of the earth."

The third reason I have hope for the Middle East is because . . .

The People of God Are Unstoppable!

God is raising up a church in the Middle East today that knows no limits when it comes to commitment and faithfulness. I just received a phone call from a church leader in the Middle East. When I told him I was working on the book he has been praying for, he said, "Tell the people who will read your book that we believers in the Middle East are ready to die for Jesus!"

His words reminded me of the Iranian believers who quote Esther's statement "If I die, I die" whenever they go out to minister in the dangerous nation of Iran. God can do a lot with that kind of commitment. Take heart, church! Turn off the news, and take your worldview from the pages of Scripture—and you'll have more hope.

The Power of God Is Unlimited!

The Plan of God Is Unending!

The People of God Are Unstoppable!

The Charge

Today more than ever Jesus' church needs to answer the call to fulfill the Great Commission. Muslims around the world are normal people, created in the image of God. They are warm, friendly, and gracious. Unfortunately, because of terrorism all Muslims are often painted as something less than human. As with any people group or religion, we can't just lump everyone into one category or stereotype. The majority of Muslims don't want jihad. As I said at the beginning of this book, they just want to feed their children, send them to good schools, see them get married, and then have lots of grandchildren.

Nevertheless, we live in the most dangerous time the world has ever known. Hard-line Islamic forces threaten the very existence of civilization. I have tried to pull no punches in this book. I want to be honest and forthright about the history of Islam and how jihadists like Hamas, Hezbollah, Islamic Jihad, and al-Qaeda and nations like Iran, Syria, and Saudi Arabia want to return to the glory days of world domination. None of this can be minimized, and the West continues to be asleep at the wheel while the danger grows to epic proportions.

I believe the only solution to this desperate situation is Jesus. We have seen peace plans and peace treaties come and go in the Middle East. Jesus, however, can set all people free from their sin and bitterness—if they have the opportunity to hear his message. This certainly includes Muslims, as we have seen scores of Arabs, Persians, Turks, and Kurds receive this freedom that only Jesus can give. We also have seen the reconciliation that occurs when a Jew receives Jesus as his Savior and then the love of God fills his heart for the Palestinians. God's love is for all people; it does not discriminate. We have seen former terrorists in the Middle East lay down their weapons and pick up a Bible. No one is beyond the love of Christ. No one is unreachable.

If the church continues to bring the message of Jesus into the heart of the Islamic world, the people will respond; and the region, along with the rest of the world, will be changed. This spiritual revolution has already begun, and it is growing every day. What's more, you can be a part of it. So turn off the news, get into the Word of God, get on your knees, and join the revolution. Jesus is bringing the good news to the Middle East, and those who live there will never be the same. Want to join us? The next chapter will tell you how.

Henry Martyn
—First Missionary to the Muslims

Henry Martyn (1781–1812) was part of the golden age of world missions. William Carey, who is called the "father of modern missions," helped ignite a missionary movement through his inspirational preaching and his willingness to go to India during this period. Adoniram and Nancy Judson also served Christ courageously during this era. Thirteen days after getting married they sailed to Calcutta. Adoniram later translated the New Testament into Burmese. Accused of being a British spy, he was imprisoned for seventeen months when war broke out between England and Burma. His wife died soon afterward, but he kept serving the Lord in Burma.

Henry Martyn was born in England, where he served briefly as an Anglican priest. Wanting to be a missionary, he first went to India. But Martyn is perhaps best remembered for his work in Persia. He is known as the first Protestant missionary to the Muslim world. Though Martyn died at age thirty-one, how much this man of God accomplished in such a short life! He suffered from poor health for the majority of his time on the mission field. He wrote in his diary during the voyage to India, "Now let me burn out for God." I believe God was able to use Martyn greatly because of the way he structured his life. He spent several hours each day in prayer and devotion to God.

Despite the countless needs in central Asia, Martyn centered his life on God—and kept it that way.[7]

In his book *Healing the Broken Family of Abraham*, Don McCurry salutes Henry Martyn. A learned man, he was trained at Cambridge University and eventually could speak Urdu, Persian, Arabic, Sanskrit, and Hindustani. Though he died at thirty-one, he "burned out for God" as he had hoped. During his short missionary service he translated the New Testament into three languages: Persian, Arabic, and Hindustani. He wrote tracts. He debated Muslims. He developed seven principles for working with Muslims, which—two hundred years later—are still effective.

Henry Martyn's Seven Principles to Reach Muslims

1. Share your own personal experience—your testimony of how you experienced the forgiveness of sins and peace with God through Jesus Christ.

2. Appreciate the best in your Muslim friend and ascribe such qualities to God working in his life. The same could go for those elements in Muslim culture that are genuinely approved by God.

3. Keep your message Christ-centered, as you talk about the grace of God and how it is mediated through Christ and carried forward by the sanctifying work of God's Spirit.

---

7. Ruth Tucker, *From Jerusalem to Irian Jaya: A Biographical History of Christian Missions* (Grand Rapids: Zondervan, 1983), 132–34.

4. Draw your Muslim friend into the study of the Scriptures so that he can discover these new truths for himself.

5. Play the role of a supporting friend as your Muslim friend goes through this time of critical investigation and decision-making.

6. Create a favorable atmosphere in society by ministering to human needs.

7. Trust the Holy Spirit to work in your Muslim friend as he seeks his place as a believer in his Muslim context.[8]

8. Don McCurry, *Healing the Broken Family of Abraham: New Life for Muslims* (Colorado Springs: Ministries to Muslims Publishing, 2001), 177–78.

11

The Prayer Revolution

I am convinced that one of the reasons—perhaps the *greatest* reason—we have seen so many Muslims come to faith in Christ in the last few years is because of the fervent prayers of believers around the world.

There is no question that God Almighty has unlimited power that can be summoned at a moment's notice to reach those who need him so desperately. His Word, the Bible, has been translated into the language of the vast majority of Muslim people; and Muslims who are willing to read it have been transformed by being exposed to the truth that can set them free. God our Father has also equipped and used Christian ministry leaders and believers in the Middle East who have been faithful to stand in the midst of persecution with the inviting message of love for all Muslims. God has also used dreams, visions, and other dramatic experiences to open the hearts of Muslims who would not have considered Jesus otherwise.

The most important thing you can do for the Muslims of the world is to pray for them. Here are a few websites that promote prayer for people of the Muslim world.

www.30daysprayer.com/muslim

www.gospelformuslims.com

www.e3partners.org

Now let's look at five key prayer targets within the Muslim world that need our urgent and faithful intercession today.

Prayer Target #1: Christian Leaders and Their Families

Pastors and Christian workers in the Muslim world live under constant and extreme pressure. Yet they are willing to sacrifice everything—even their lives, if necessary—in order to bring the light to those in darkness. One pastor who has been to prison and has had to move many times because of threats against both himself and his family recently told me, "I have, more than a few times, answered my cell phone to the sound of gunshots in the background as a warning for me to stop telling Muslims about Jesus. I don't fear for my own life, but I must confess that I am anxious about my wife and small children."

I asked him how he is able to continue to live under this daily pressure. "It's because of three words found in Colossians 1:27," he replied. "*Christ in you.* To me, these are the three most important words in the Christian life. If you read the first chapter of Colossians, the magnitude of what Christ has done for us is hard to fathom. It's difficult to even grasp a portion of it."

By him all things were created: things in heaven and on earth, visible and invisible, whether thrones or powers or rulers or authorities; all things were created by him and for him. He is before all things, and in him all things hold together. And he is the head of the body, the church; he is the beginning and the firstborn from among the dead, so that in everything he might have the supremacy. For God was pleased to have all his fullness dwell in him, and through him to reconcile to himself all things, whether things on earth or things in heaven, by making peace through his blood, shed on the cross. (Colossians 1:16–20)

My friend continued: "When we see that Christ is over all of creation, then how can we possibly grasp that he *lives in us*? This is too amazing. So we can never wonder where we receive the strength to live for Jesus in the midst of persecution. He is giving us the ability to do this each day."

Because of the pressure upon them and their families, Christian pastors and leaders, like so many others, could simply leave the Middle East and find a safer and more comfortable place to live. One pastor in the Middle East was offered a pastorate, with a healthy salary, in a beautiful area of Southern California. He chose to stay. More Muslims will be in heaven, no doubt, because of his decision.

Let's commit to pray for Christian leaders and their families in the Muslim world.

Prayer Target #2:
Believers in General

Can you imagine living where your family's safety is in jeopardy and continually deciding whether or not to remain there? That's what believers in Muslim nations face. Whether it's in the Gaza Strip, Afghanistan, or Iran, the desire to just get out of there and live somewhere else is always present. When I'm in the Middle East, I can easily see how tempting it would be to throw up your hands and say, "I'm out of here!" But so many don't do that.

One day my wife, JoAnn, said to me, "Have you ever noticed that the believers in the Muslim world never ask God to end their trials? They ask God to teach them what they need to learn while in the midst of the trials—and that's it!"

As I mentioned earlier, I have to confess that when I'm in a trial my first prayer is for God to get me out of it. That's the extent of my prayers. *Get it over with, Lord—and please do it today!*

Over the last twelve years I've had the privilege of taking about 750 people to the Middle East. One of the most frequently asked questions is "How do the Christians weather all of the trials?" There is always war—or the threat of it just around the corner. Persecution constantly looms for believers living within reach of Islamic fundamentalists. Living conditions are often difficult; in some areas families eat only one meal a day.

I was in the Gaza Strip one time with Jason Elam, who has been a kicker in the National Football League for many years. While we were there, we got caught in the middle of a major confrontation between Hamas and the Israel Defense Forces. For four days Gaza was bombed every three minutes. In between the bombings, missiles were being shot out of the Strip into Israel. The noise was so loud that it was hard to think. There was no electricity, and the people were able to eat only one meal a day. Yet despite all of that, not one meeting was canceled at the church in Gaza. No one even talked about the terrible situation. There were more important things to do—like worship God.

It's hard for most of us to imagine living for even one day like believers do in the Muslim world. Let's pray for these believers who live for Jesus in the midst of such trying circumstances.

Prayer Target #3: Muslims to Embrace Christ

Throughout *Breakthrough* you've read the stories of Muslims in the Middle East accepting Jesus as their Savior. And now I invite you to be a part of this important time in history. Muslims are open, ready, and waiting for the gospel. Here is an easy way to pray for them: each time you watch the news and hear a Muslim country mentioned or see breaking news pertaining to a Muslim nation go by on the ticker tape, pray for God to open the people's hearts to Christ. It's that simple. The place where the most conflict is occurring is probably the place that needs the most prayer.

So when you hear about Iran, Afghanistan, Iraq, Syria, Egypt, Lebanon, the Gaza Strip, or Israel, pray for God to open the hearts of the people. That's where the spiritual war is occurring. Those are the places that need to be covered in prayer.

Prayer Target #4:
The Nations in the Islamic World

We have put together a tool to help you pray each week for one nation that has a significant Muslim population.

A Prayer Guide for the Muslim World

The following chart lists fifty-two countries. The total number of Muslims in these nations is over one billion. Most of these nations have a population that is at least 50 percent Muslim; the others, while not having a Muslim-majority population, still have a significant number of Muslims.

By using this chart as a guide, you will intercede for one country every week. In one year you will have covered a majority of Muslims around the world. Here are some suggested ways to pray for each nation:

- for hearts to be open to the gospel
- for believers to remain faithful and bold
- for individuals and entire families to come to Christ
- for solid discipleship of new believers
- for strong new churches in which new believers can grow in their faith
- for Jesus to use his church to radically change the nation

52 Weeks of Prayer for the Muslim World

Country	Muslim Population	Percentage of Total Pop.
1. Indonesia	195,272,000	86%
2. Pakistan	160,272,000	97%
3. India	154,500,000	13%
4. Bangladesh	129,681,509	83%
5. Turkey	72,750,000	99%
6. Egypt	69,560,000	90%
7. Iran	68,805,000	98%
8. Nigeria	65,750,000	50%
9. Algeria	32,472,000	99%
10. Morocco	30,393,000	99%
11. Afghanistan	29,601,000	99%
12. Sudan	29,346,000	70%
13. Iraq	27,936,000	97%
14. Saudi Arabia	24,600,000	99%
15. Ethiopia	24,471,842	33%
16. Uzbekistan	23,232,000	88%
17. Yemen	20,680,000	99%
18. China	20,000,000	1.5%
19. Tanzania	18,250,000	35%
20. Syria	16,560,000	90%
21. Russia	15,250,000	14%
22. Malaysia	14,030,000	61%
23. Niger	13,580,000	80%
24. Senegal	10,998,000	94%
25. Ivory Coast	10,920,000	60%
26. Ghana	9,900,000	16%

27. Tunisia	9,800,000	98%
28. Somalia	8,600,000	99%
29. Azerbaijan	8,567,000	93%
30. Guinea	8,075,000	85%
31. Kazakhstan	7,097,000	47%
32. Burkina Faso	6,950,000	50%
33. Tajikistan	6,120,000	90%
34. France	5,980,000	8.5%
35. Libya	5,626,000	97%
36. Israel*	5,000,000	46%
37. Turkmenistan	4,628,000	89%
38. United Arab Emirates	4,416,000	96%
39. Kenya	3,700,000	10%
40. Mauritania	3,100,000	99%
41. Germany	3,060,000	4%
42. United States	3,000,000	1%
43. Oman	2,376,000	75%
44. Albania	2,120,000	70%
45. Lebanon	2,104,000	59%
46. Serbia, Montenegro, Kosovo region	2,030,000	19%
47. Benin	1,680,000	24%
48. South Africa	938,000	2%
49. Djibouti	752,000	94%
50. Bahrain	700,000	81%
51. Western Sahara	300,000	99%
52. Maldives	300,000	99%

* Figures for Israel include the Gaza Strip and the West Bank

Finding accurate population numbers is difficult, especially in relation to religion. I arrived at most of the totals above by comparing the CIA World Factbook (https://www.cia.gov/library/publications/the-world-factbook) and Wikipedia (http://en.wikipedia.org). In some cases the chart represents government-released figures; in other cases the numbers are estimates. No one but God, who is omniscient, knows the totals for certain. We know that in some nations there are many believers who, because of persecution, have gone underground. I also think it's clear that a great number of Muslims are Muslim in name only. I believe, therefore, that most of these numbers are on the high side. It is my hope that this chart won't just represent numbers to you, but individual people who need Jesus Christ.

Prayer Target #5: The Women of the Muslim World

Since the Muslim world is quite diverse, women's rights vary from country to country. If a woman lives under Sharia law in Iran, she will have few rights, if any. Most Islamic countries are at least influenced by Sharia law. Women may enjoy more rights in a place like Jordan than in Iran, as there is a more modern outlook on life that allows women more freedom. But that wouldn't be the case in the more fundamentalist areas even within the more progressive countries.

My wife, JoAnn, has an overflowing heart for these women, and she has started a women's ministry called Selah. Here are her thoughts about women in the Muslim world:

"Freedom" and "choice" are not words to which Muslim women can relate. Sharia law makes the decisions for the majority of women in the Middle East. They know how they are expected to dress: their heads (and possibly faces) covered, their arms and legs also unexposed. And they know what the punishment will be if they break the dress code. In some countries they can actually be put to death for exposing those parts of their bodies.

Most women in the Middle East are told whom they will marry—perhaps a first or second cousin, or maybe a man as much as thirty years her senior. I have met many believers who wouldn't have chosen to marry their husbands. When asked if they love their husbands, a common answer is, "He is a good man."

According to women's rights advocates, the literacy rate for Middle East women is 46.2 percent. And even though men can marry more than one woman, in countries like Iran they almost automatically get custody of the children after a divorce.[1]

Not only are women told what to do and how to do it, but they are often treated as inferior to men. When a baby boy is born, there is much rejoicing; when a baby girl is born, there is grieving. Men are honored; women are not. This thinking influences how a woman views herself—as unworthy and unvalued and unloved. Combine this with the high incidents of abuse, rape, and beatings; and you can imagine the lives these women are forced to live. Because of shame, women will carry these hurts inside their hearts, never sharing their pain with anyone else. Yet when they hear the good news of Jesus Christ and trust him alone for salvation, they can experience unconditional love.

Galatians 3:28 is such a powerful passage for women

---

1. Xin Li, "Iranian Women's Rights Severely Restricted," *Washington Times*, March 8, 2006.

in the Muslim world: "There is neither Jew nor Greek, slave nor free, *male nor female*, for you are all one in Christ Jesus" (emphasis added). God declares in this epistle that men and women are equal in essence to him. We may have different functions in life, but men and women have the same value in God's eyes. How revolutionary this is in Islamic societies.

Women in the Middle East are tenderhearted, humble, and generous; they love others unconditionally. The Lord has given me a heart of compassion for his daughters in the Middle East. My desire is to come alongside them as a sister of equal value, loving them and honoring them. As I build friendships with them, trust is formed. When trust is present and they feel secure, then they begin share deeply about their lives.

Prayer is a strong tool that the Holy Spirit uses to break down the walls erected around the human heart. As women bring their pain into the light, God miraculously begins to heal those deep hurts. Please pray for the women of the Muslim world. They are raising the next generation. If they are reached for Christ, their influence could transform the people of the Middle East and beyond.

There you have it. Urgent, targeted prayer is needed in the Muslim world for

- Christian leaders and their families
- Believers in general
- Muslims to embrace Christ
- The nations in the Islamic world
- The women of the Muslim world

Breakthrough:
The Return of Hope to the Middle East

This book was written to inform you, inspire you, and challenge you to action. There *is* good news from the Middle East today; there *is* cause for hope and rejoicing. God is moving among the Muslim people there.

As believers in Christ Jesus, we are called to reach the world. But before we can do that, I am convinced we must be able to see the world through the world's eyes. We must, without a spirit of judgment, understand people for who they are. We must empathize with Muslims and learn how they think. That will occur as God fills our hearts with love for them. Muslims need Jesus just like you and me and everyone else in the world.

So my prayer is that God will fill your heart with love for the Muslim people. And by the way, I am not alone in this prayer. *A prayer team has been praying for you as you were reading this book.* They have been asking God to open your heart and put within you a love for the people of Islam like you have never experienced before. They too have this love for Muslims. You see, all the members of this prayer team live in the midst of the Muslim world themselves. You may not have met them personally, but you already know them. The people praying for you are the people you have met in this book. They want you to know they are thrilled that you now know their stories. These amazing believers asked me to deliver a message to you. "Tell them that we love them as our brothers and sisters in Christ, and we invite them to pray for us too."

There is a breakthrough—the return of hope to the Middle East. God is moving among Muslims and Jews more today than ever before. And now that you know some of their stories and are connected to these believers through prayer, you are a part of the breakthrough too. You will play a vital part from now on. Your prayers will join with the prayers of the saints in the Muslim world, and together we will have the privilege of watching our Father in heaven reach more Muslims and Jews for Christ. Our great hope and confidence as believers is that one day we will all meet together in heaven around the throne of God. Now that will be a celebration! Pray without ceasing!

Welcome to the team,

Tom Doyle